THE PALESTINIAN RIGHT OF RETURN UNDER INTERNATIONAL LAW

THE
PALESTINIAN
RIGHT OF RETURN
UNDER
INTERNATIONAL
LAW

FRANCIS A. BOYLE

CLARITY PRESS, INC.

© 2011 Francis A. Boyle

ISBN: 0-932863-93-0
     978-0-932863-93-5

In-house editor: Diana G. Collier
Cover: R. Jordan P. Santos
Cover photo: activestills.org

Clarity Press, Inc.
Ste. 469, 3277 Roswell Rd. NE
Atlanta, GA. 30305 , USA
http://www.claritypress.com

In Memory of my Grandfather
George Andrew Monarque II
who in 1947 was the first person
in the Boyle/Monarque Family
to care about the Palestinians:
"But what about the poor Arabs?"

R. I. P.

International lawyer Francis A. Boyle (far left) on the floor of the World Court in 1993, squaring off against his adversary, Shabtai Rosenne (far right) from the Jewish Bantustan (aka Israel) representing the genocidal Yugoslavia, just before he argued and then won the first of his two World Court Orders for Bosnia on the basis of the 1948 Genocide Convention. (See Trying to Stop Aggressive War and Genocide against the People and the Republic of Bosnia and Hezegovina in Appendix 2.)

Francis Boyle took the case of Bosnia to the International Court of Justice in The Hague in 1993, winning two Orders for provisional measures of protection against the genocidal Yugoslavia in favor of Bosnia and Herzegovina.

Francis A. Boyle meeting with Palestinian President Yasser Arafat at the Presidential Compound in Gaza in December 1997, in order to celebrate the Tenth Anniversary of the First Palestinian Intifada that started in Gaza and led directly to the 1988 Palestinian Declaration of Independence, for which he served as Legal Advisor.

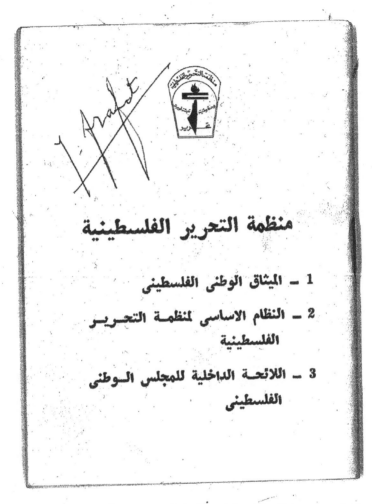

منظمة التحرير الفلسطينية

1 ــ الميثاق الوطنى الفلسطينى

2 ــ النظام الاساسى لمنظمة التحرير الفلسطينية

3 ــ اللائحة الداخلية للمجلس الوطنى الفلسطينى

At their 1997 Gaza meeting, President Arafat presented Francis A. Boyle with a personally inscribed copy of the 1988 Palestinian Declaration of Independence, for which he served as Legal Advisor.

TABLE OF CONTENTS

Introduction

Addressing the Right of Return of the Palestinian people, U.N. General Assembly Resolution 194 (III) of 1948 unequivocally:

> *Resolves* that the refugees wishing to return to their homes and live at peace with their neighbours should be permitted to do so at the earliest practicable date, and that compensation should be paid for the property of those choosing not to return and for loss of damage to property which, under principles of international law or in equity, should be made good by the Governments or authorities responsible...

Under the auspices of the Obama administration, in September 2010 direct Middle East peace negotiations on the so-called final status issues resumed between the Israelis and the Palestinians after they had been maliciously disrupted by Israeli's barbaric and genocidal "Operation Cast Lead" against Gaza from December 27, 2008 to January 18, 2009. This latest Israeli extermination campaign murdered about 1400 Palestinians, 80% of whom were civilians, by means of high-tech weapon systems and political support provided by the Bush Jr. administration without even one word of public criticism uttered by then incoming President-elect Obama. Today it appears that what the Obama administration has in mind is the coerced imposition of a self-styled comprehensive peace settlement upon the Palestinians (1) that will force them to accept a Bantustan of disjointed and surrounded chunks of territory on the West Bank and Gaza; (2) that will compel the Palestinians to expressly recognize Israel as "the Jewish State"; and (3) that will force the Palestinians to give up their well-recognized Right of Return under United Nations General Assembly Resolution 194(III) of 1948. Of course this type of arrangement will not work for the reasons so powerfully and eloquently stated by Dr. Haidar Abdul Shaffi and Dr. Hanan Ashrawi herein.

The late Dr. Haidar Abdul Shaffi was Chair of the Palestinian Delegation to the Middle East Peace Negotiations from 1991 to 1993, that is, from Madrid to Oslo. Dr. Hanan Ashrawi was the Spokesperson for the Palestinian Delegation to the Middle East Peace Negotiations during that time. I served as Legal Advisor to the Palestinian Delegation to the Middle East Peace Negotiations from 1991 to 1993, giving advice, counsel, and assistance to Dr. Haidar and to Dr. Hanan—as they are affectionately called by Palestinians all over the world.

Earlier, at the Camp David II Middle East Peace Negotiations convened under the auspices of the Clinton administration for the summer of 2000, all three of us had been confronted with an identical situation, namely: the United States government and Israel attempted to terminate the recognized right of the Palestinian refugees to return to their homes in exchange for nothing more than a Palestinian Bantustan on the West Bank and Gaza. So in order to head off this second catastrophe, the Council for Palestinian Restitution and Repatriation organized two separate press conferences in Washington, D.C., one for Dr. Haidar and one for Dr. Hanan, with me once again serving as their Counsel. The purpose of this exercise was for us collectively to send the strongest message possible to the United States government and to the Israeli government that there will be no peace in the Middle East unless they recognize the right of return for Palestinian refugees in accordance with Resolution 194.

Chapter One sets forth the slightly edited comments made by Dr. Hanan and me at our seminal press conference on March 3, 2000. Chapter Two sets forth the slightly edited comments made by Dr. Haidar and me at our seminal press conference on April 21, 2000. With specific reference to the Palestinian Right of Return under international law, absolutely nothing has changed legally, politically, or diplomatically since these incredibly powerful and eloquent statements made by Dr. Haidar and Dr. Hanan.

There has been an enormous amount of scholarly literature generated on the Palestinian Right of Return under International Law by professors. But nothing in that corpus is as genuine, authentic, powerful, personal, or convincing as these two press conferences held by Dr. Haidar and by Dr. Hanan. They are two of the best and the brightest that occupied Palestine has to offer—Dr. Haidar having lived in Gaza; Dr. Hanan from the West Bank. Neither Dr. Haidar nor Dr. Hanan were professional politicians or diplomats or lawyers. Rather they were both genuine grassroots leaders of the Palestinian people living under the boot of one of the most brutal, colonial, genocidal, military occupation regimes in the post World War II era. Both rose to prominence because of their own personal courage, integrity, principles, guts, and determination. They literally put their lives on the line for their people in order to resist the Machiavellian machinations by Israel and the United States of America.

Whatever the Obama administration might say or think it is undertaking, there will be no peace in the Middle East unless these peace negotiations recognize, and deal in good faith with, the right of the Palestinian refugees to return to their homes for the reasons explained by Dr. Haidar and Dr. Hanan in this book. Their prophetic words still apply in spades today! The reader must study these seminal press statements by Dr. Haidar and by Dr. Hanan in order to understand why the realization of the Palestinian Right of Return goes to the very heart of the Middle East Peace Process between the Israelis and the Palestinians. Continued failure and refusal by the governments of the United States and Israel to heed these profound words of wisdom by Dr. Haidar and Dr. Hanan will only spell at least another generation of violence, bloodshed, and tears between Israelis and Palestinians.

The Conclusion to this book respectfully sets forth my newest, sincere, and good faith advice to the Palestinian people that they might consider what to do now in light of the manifest, longstanding and unremitting campaign of violence, criminality, and sheer depravity perpetrated against them by Israel since the 1948 *Nakba* (Catastrophe) propelled so many Palestinians into their now semi-permanent exile from home: ***Sign nothing and let Israel collapse in Palestine!*** That is the ultimate solution for fulfilling the Palestinian Right of Return under International Law.

The "State" of Israel has never been anything but a Bantustan for Jews that was established in Palestine after the Second World War by the White racist and genocidal Western colonial imperial powers in order to control and dominate the Middle East at their behest. As such this Jewish Bantustan will suffer the same terminal fate as did the Bantustans for Blacks founded by the White racist criminal apartheid regime in South Africa and for the same reasons. Consequently, the Palestinians must sign no peace treaty with this apartheid Jewish Bantustan and let it collapse of its own racist and genocidal weight. In this regard, my former adversary the genocidal Yugoslavia collapsed as a State, lost its U.N. membership, and no longer exists as a State. The same fate will happen to the genocidal Bantustan for Jews known as "Israel." It is only a matter of time.

This latest recommendation to the Palestinian people is based upon my personal involvement with their struggle since January of 1970. That history is chronicled in Appendix 1 to this book. It contains the first of my two 18th Annual Bertrand Russell Peace Lectures I delivered at MacMaster University in Canada on January 9, 2007 under the overall theme of *The Legacy of Bertrand Russell: Principle Confronting Power.* Toward that end, this book has been published.

Chapter One

The Palestinian Right of Return with Dr. Hanan Ashrawi

CPRR Press Release 28/02/2000
For immediate release
28 February 2000

PALESTINIANS UNITED
ON RIGHTS TO RETURN AND RESTITUTION

While Israel continues to deny the human rights of Palestinian refugees, more than fifteen thousand Palestinians and their supporters from all over the world have signed a petition reaffirming that every Palestinian has a legitimate, individual right of return to his or her original home and to absolute restitution of all of his or her property.

The petition was initiated on 21 January 2000 by the Council for Palestinian Restitution and Repatriation (CPRR), a non-profit, non-partisan, non-governmental organization dedicated to providing legal aid to Palestinians and their heirs to achieve their legitimate rights. The campaign is intended to reflect the united voice of the Palestinian people and their resolve to never allow these basic human rights to be abrogated in any way. Some 150 organizations in Palestine and around the world have endorsed the petition and affiliated with CPRR calling on all Palestinians, non-governmental organizations, and people of conscience to join this campaign. This unity among Palestinians can be clearly seen from the fact that prominent Palestinians from Palestine and the Diaspora reflecting various political, social, and religious backgrounds have signed and support the petition, including Haidar Abdul-Shaffi, Ibrahim Abu Lughod, Basel Aql, Naseer Aruri, Hanan Ashrawi, Fateh Azzam, Burhan Dajani, Waheed El-Hamdalla, Mohammad Hallaj, Shafiq al-Hout, Bishop Samir Kafity, Said Khoury, Hassan Khreishe, Eugene Makhlouf, Mu'awiye Masri, Fouad Moughrabi, Abdul Sattar Qasem, Ahmad Qatamesh, Abdel Muhsin Qattan, Hasib

Sabbagh, Edward Said, Abdel Jawad Saleh, Bassam Shaka'a, Fakhri Fahed Turkuman, and Marouf Zahran.

The rights of Palestinians to their land and property are inalienable individual human rights decreed by the Universal Declaration of Human Rights. The right to return means the return of Palestinian refugees to their homes, lands, villages, and towns of origin, including to their actual houses, where these still stand. These two rights cannot nullify one another.

CPRR will organize a series of periodical press conferences by prominent members of the Palestinian community from all political, social and religious backgrounds to highlight the unity of all Palestinians on the fundamental rights of restitution and repatriation. Eventually the petition will be sent to all the parties involved, including Israel, the Palestine Liberation Organization (PLO), the Palestinian Authority (PA), the United States, the European Union, the Russian Federation, and to the international community. In addition copies of the petition will be made available to a wide range of international institutions and organizations, including the international media.

Council for Palestinian Restitution and Reparation
News Conference
on Palestinian Refugees
Washington, DC
March 3, 2000

MR. JAWDAT HINDI: Ladies and gentlemen, I present myself as one of the few lucky persons who had a chance to live after Tantura the massacre that is now documented by an Israeli professor. And I hope that you got your copies of that. I was born in Tantura. Tantura is a small village 24 kilometers to the south of Haifa, a coastal village with inhabitants not more than 2,000. I was born in 1926. The people lived happily and with good relations with their neighbors, inhabitants of the old settlement, the Haron Jericho, which was not more than 14 kilometers from Tantura. In April 1948, Haifa was occupied by the Zionists. And all the people of Palestine and especially the places that were not far away from Haifa, they tried to find something—a solution to themselves. The people of my village decided to keep good relations with the Jews, their neighbors, but at the same time to protect themselves and to defend their village if they are attacked by Zionists.

Twenty-second and twenty-third of May 1948, the people had a normal day. Farmers went to their land, came back to their homes, fishermen—because it is a coastal village—came back. And everybody went to his bed, and we were thinking that nothing will happen to us. After 12 midnight—I speak of myself and my family. My father had passed away years before and I was the eldest, so I lived with my mother and sisters and brothers. We walked upstairs—explosions and the house was shaking. Showers of rapid fire and so many things. And we didn't know what to do. Then we rushed out of the house. We met our neighbors coming this way and that way, and we were talking. And everybody was concerned of the 30 young men who were guarding us, because the village had in that time only 30 rifles and 30 men were every night escorting us. And we thought ourselves in our homes safe.

Then, an old man advised us to go back to our homes and to lock the door as well. We went. After one hour, the door was broken and soldiers rushed into our house, kicking with their boots, pointing their guns into our heads. All of us were scared. But I am—being the eldest, I looked at the youngest—how they were scared. Then they pushed us out of the house. We went out and we found that the neighbors are coming this way and that way—the same like the soldiers did to us. And we gathered in an open place. And we waited there, the soldiers laughing, hugging each other.

And all of a sudden, a family was coming from out of the side. And suddenly we heard shooting and we looked there and all the members of that family fell down—parents and children. And then they drove us. And we went through the roads—bodies here and there, killed people, men, children, women—and we were gathered in at the seashore in front of a high building. There they separated the women from men, and they ordered us to sit down and to raise our hands over our heads and not to look up but to look down.

After maybe 15 minutes, an officer came. And by signaling to us to raise our faces and to look at him. And he started pointing with his fingers: you, you, you, you, and doing the same signal just to let them know to come out. Ten people were gathered. Then he talked in his own language. And four soldiers came and pointed their guns to the backs of the 10 men and they drove them away—where to we didn't know. Another official came and the same happened. Ten people were gathered and four soldiers that drove them back. The third time. The fourth time, I was called out. But they didn't call anybody else.

Then the officer talked to two soldiers. I didn't understand what did he say. Then they pushed me and one said in a broken Arabic: "Your home, your home." What I understood that they wanted to come to my home. So I led them there. When we reached our home, soldiers were there, eating and drinking, laughing. And the two soldiers came into the house. They started searching every corner of the house. They found nothing. Then they drove me back. We passed a narrow lane, a narrow road. The two soldiers started fighting each other. I didn't know why. Then one of them pointed his gun into my head. The other pushed him and said in his language—(speaks in foreign language). Anyway, at last they pushed me and we went back to the place where the people are gathered. They talked to their officer. The officer told me to sit down. I sat down. That man who had been pointing his gun to my head—he wanted to kill me. And he didn't. He kicked me with his boot and spat into my face. After one hour—you can say that from sunrise up till four in the afternoon—they started searching the women and children - - infants. And they took all their jewelries and money.

Then they drove them into trucks and then to a nearby village called Fouradis, a village which was occupied by the Jews, and the second day—or it might be the first week, I'm not sure of that, but not more than days—they took all the people, all the women and children into the border area to Karan city, the nearest town from a place— Natania as I remember was the name of that. Anyway, for the women after one hour they came also and drove us in trucks to the Throne Jacob. This is the nearby settlement. There was a police station—a big one. And they pushed us into that station. And we stayed the night there in the prison and in some open spaces. We stayed there that night.

Then they took us to a deserted Arab village called Emhalit. And the houses were demolished. Some of the houses were still, and they kept us there. Then by force—beating us—we put the wires around the whole village and worked for a whole week to make our own prison. And this was called prisoners of war camp.

Now what about those groups of 10 people who were guarded and then four soldiers—they were driving 10 people and so on? When we met in the Throne Jacob that night, the first time I heard about that. The four soldiers drove the 10 men. And they ordered them to pull the bodies of the killed people and then ordered them to dig a big hole and to drag the bodies into that hole. Then they ordered eight of them to stand around the opening of the hole. And then they started shooting at them and the eight fell into the same hole that they had digged. Then they ordered the two – [starts crying]—excuse me—and then they ordered the two who were saved to cover the bodies. And then they drove them back to where we were gathered, just to tell what happened.

Four groups of 10 people were taken before they took me. How many did they take after that? I don't know. But for sure, there were many. And at the same time, no weapons at all were with the people in their houses. All what we had—30 guards—and they were at the borders of the village. But they started shooting in the roads, in the houses and so on.

So after these days, maybe last month, I heard that an Israeli professor is documenting our massacre and at the same time so many channels of the news had reviewed that. We stayed in there as prisoners of war for a long time. And I forgot my name. They called me in that time—[speaks in Arabic]—Prisoner of War Number 3310. Then they started the exchange of prisoners of war with Jordan. Their soldiers came back to them. But why did they push us to Jordan as exchanging their prisoners? We were not Jordanians, but they pushed us to Jordan. Why they didn't let us go back to our homes, our mothers, wives, children—they were expelled before us and we were pushed out.

Really when I came Tantura—I met the people of Tantura – most of them are refugees still in camps in Syria. Me and my brother, when we went out direct we went to Syria, and then we found that—for my good luck, for we were fortunate—an uncle who was in Lebanon, in Beirut. He studied—he was a physician after studying in American University there. And he stayed in Lebanon. He came to Damascus and took his sister, my mother, brothers and sisters and lived with them. So we came to Beirut, lived four months and then we went to Syria and worked there. And then I worked in Kuwait and I came 1988 to the United States and I am now a United States citizen. And thank you very much.

MR. BOYLE: Thank you, Mr. Hindi, for that very moving story. Having worked with the Palestinian people for the last 20 years, I can assure you there are enormous numbers of stories that are just as tragic and compelling as the one we heard from Mr. Hindi.

As you know, the final status negotiations have now begun in theory with respect to the Middle East. And the right of Palestinian refugees to return to their homes is a critical issue. There are over five million Palestinian refugees around the world, as well as internally displaced people. Before I introduce our keynote speaker, I've been asked to say a few words about their legal rights.*

As a condition for its admission to the United Nations Organization, Israel formally agreed to accept General Assembly Resolution 181 of 1947, dealing with the partition of the mandate for Palestine into two states, a Jewish state and a Palestinian state, as well as an international trusteeship for the city of Jerusalem. And Israel also

---

* See Francis A. Boyle, *A New Direction for the Palestinian People*, reprinted below.

expressly agreed to accept Resolution 194 of 1948—the Palestinian Right of Return. And let me just read you the critical paragraph. Again, this is what Israel accepted as a condition for its admission to the United Nations Organization, and I quote: "Resolves that the refugees wishing to return to their homes and live at peace with their neighbors should be permitted to do so at the earliest practicable date and that compensation should be paid for the property of those choosing not to return and for loss of or damage to property which under principles of international law or in equity should be made good by the governments or authorities responsible."

Now, Prime Minister Barak has recently stated that he would not tolerate the return of any Palestinian refugees to their homes. What do we say to Prime Minister Barak? That if he carries out that illegal policy, he jeopardizes Israel's continued participation in the activities of the United Nations General Assembly. If Prime Minister Barak is going to deny the right of the Palestinian refugees to return to their homes, he will abrogate and violate one of the most important conditions for Israel's admission to the United Nations. And this could produce the most severe consequences for Israel. They could be suspended from participation in the United Nations by the General Assembly—exactly what the General Assembly did to the genocidal Yugoslavia and to the South African government under the apartheid regime.[1]

Now, we've spent a lot of time here in the United States for many years arguing that Soviet Jews had a right of family reunification, and that those Soviet Jews being kept in the Soviet Union against their wishes had a right to leave and join their families. And that was the correct position to take, and the United States government repeatedly invoked Article 13, Paragraph 2 of the 1948 Universal Declaration of Human Rights on behalf of Soviet Jews.[2] Well, I am invoking that same paragraph two of the Universal Declaration of Human Rights on behalf of the Palestinian refugees to return to their homes. And it says quite clearly, quote: "Everyone has the right... to return to his country." Unquote. That was as of 1948. And that supplements Resolution 194. And the United States government has consistently taken the position that that is a binding requirement of public international law. The same principle applies to the Palestinian refugees.

Just recently, historically, we've had two instances where the United States government has stood up for the rights of refugees to return to their homes. In the Dayton Agreement that was drafted by the United States government under the supervision of Richard Holbrooke, it says quite clearly that Bosnian refugees have a right to return to their homes. And of course, they do. The same principle can and must be applied to the Palestinian refugees.

And just recently, a year ago, NATO intervened in Kosovo to guarantee the right of Kosovar Albanian refugees to return to their homes. And the same principle must be applied to the Palestinian refugees. There will no peace in the Middle East unless the right of the Palestinian refugees, as recognized by Resolution 194, is implemented.

In the future course of these final status negotiations, they must be conducted on the basis of Resolution 181, Resolution 194, subsequent General Assembly resolutions and Security Council resolutions, the Third and Fourth Geneva Conventions of 1949, the 1907 Hague Regulations and other relevant principles of public international law. There is a remarkable opportunity for peace in the Middle East today – a comprehensive peace settlement. But what is needed now from the Clinton administration—which I regret to report we are not seeing, for whatever reason—is the same type of dynamic leadership and will for peace that was demonstrated by President Jimmy Carter over two decades ago. The governments of Israel and the United States must seize this historic moment for peace. Otherwise, I doubt very seriously history will give any of us a second chance for obtaining peace with justice for all peoples in the Middle East.

It is now my honor and pleasure to introduce our keynote speaker, Dr. Hanan Ashrawi. It was my great distinction to have served as the legal adviser to the Palestinian delegation to the Middle East Peace Negotiations from 1991 to 1993. That delegation was headed by Dr. Haidar Abdul-Shafi. Dr. Abdul-Shafi was not able to attend our session today because of a prior commitment. But he is on our board of directors.

The Palestinian delegation to the Middle East peace negotiations was a real people's delegation. These were not professional politicians, diplomats, and bureaucrats. These were people who represented the Palestinian people living under occupation. They were the best and the brightest that the Palestinian people—living under one of the most brutal occupations in the modern world—could offer and send to Washington, D.C. And of them all, of course, Dr. Ashrawi was selected to be the official spokesperson for the entire delegation. And in this capacity, she really became the official spokesperson for all of the Palestinian people—not only living in occupied Palestine but also in the Palestinian Diaspora.[3]

Before this, she was a professor in her own right—like me, an honorable profession—but then selected to become a diplomat and come and fight and do battle for her people, which she did most effectively, as we all know. Eventually, Dr. Ashrawi returned home. She rose to become Minister of Education in the Palestinian Authority, served for a period of time, and then decided to return to private life, where she has established her own human rights organization dedicated to the proposition of pursuing peace with justice for all in the Middle East. It's my great honor and pleasure to introduce Dr. Hanan Ashrawi.

MS. ASHRAWI: Thank you, Francis. Thank you, Jawdat. I am very glad to be here among you today. I've always maintained that spokespeople are never appointed. They are the ones who in a sense strive to represent the fullness of the humanity and existence and identity and aspirations, as well as history, of their own people. And this is the source, I believe, of anybody's credibility. But what we heard today this morning, to me, is exactly what is needed, in terms of a corrective force on a terribly flawed process. We need first the human narratives. We need to identify the victims and to recognize our humanity. And we need to correct a version of history that has constantly suffered from exclusion and denial. Because historically, when the victim speaks out, even with some personal experience and as an eyewitness and as an advocate—especially when the adversary is so powerful—the victim's narrative is often denied or distorted or confiscated or misrepresented.

And ironically, the Palestinians, like many victims, became doubly victimized because they were blamed for their victimization. So to get the narrative out and the individual identification of the human reality of what probably would have been called nowadays ethnic cleansing—one of the most tragic I wouldn't even say "incidents" but an ongoing injustice perpetrated against a whole people—a human tragedy whose extensions, repercussions, consequences we are still witnessing that has often been denied, has in many ways to be validated by an audience, by an acceptance, and most importantly, to be incorporated in any means, any attempt at solving the conflict. If we do not have a firm grasp not only of the facts and the truths and the human reality, but also the causes of the conflict itself, and if we do not attempt courageously to solve these causes, to address them directly in a candid and forthright and courageous manner, there can be no solution.

And the second most important aspect, of course, is the legal aspect. We are witnessing now attempts at negating international law to apply to the Palestinians. We are witnessing attempts, Israeli and American, to sort of make temporary transitional arrangements as the terms of reference for any solution, and thereby to bring the

Palestinians to relinquish those rights which were guaranteed to them by law, and foremost of which is the right of return. The essence of the human tragedy, of the Palestinian tragedy, is, of course, the human dimension; the fact that there was a systematic attempt at the negation, dispossession, dispersion of a whole nation and a denial of those people of their rights to natural continuity and life on their own land, of the right to their own identity, of the right to their own history, of the right to their own homes and lands. So any solution to the Palestinian question and any attempt at achieving a genuine peace has to address that core human issue from, first of all, a recognition of the facts and the identity and also firmly based on international law and legality. **We are not going to relinquish our right of return.** [Emphasis supplied.]

Many of you may say, "Well, you are not a refugee. Why do you speak out?" I'm speaking out because we are all firmly committed, first of all, to the human unity of the Palestinian people and nation. We are one people, one nation, and a solution has to address all people.

Two, as you were told, there are Palestinian refugees who are dispersed and in exile throughout the world, but there are also Palestinian refugees within Palestine. In the West Bank and Gaza we have over 1.1 million refugees, but also Palestinian refugees within what has become Israel. And these are not just displaced persons, but these are people who were forcibly, forcefully evicted from their homes. Their villages were among the 418 villages entirely demolished by Israel. And even though there were not just U.N. resolutions but even decisions within Israel to have them go back to their homes and lands, they have not been allowed to return to their homes.

We are seeing multiple dimensions and compound aspects of this human tragedy. And we are witnessing at the same time a resurgence of official denial of this tragedy, and ironically, within the context of the peace process. We are being told that issues on permanent status agenda, which are the core issues that determine not just the justice or injustice of any solution, but whether there can be a genuine peace that can lay claim to legality and to permanence, that these issues can be unilaterally prejudged and concluded by Israel, with U.S. collusion, very frankly, and at the same time with a distortion of the law. So when we look at permanent status agenda, we have the issue of Palestinian refugees. We have the issue of Jerusalem. We have the issue of boundaries, core settlements that are illegally built on Palestinian land, and then other issues pertaining to water rights and external relations and security.

Without something addressing and recognizing the Palestinian refugee question, there can be no solution. We are not interested in appeasement. We are not interested in a temporary truce. We are interested in a historical reconciliation. For that to take place, every individual narrative, not just Jawdat's narratives, has to be validated, acknowledged and affirmed, and the instruments for the solution of this very human tragedy have to be put in place. This is the historical redemptive part. If we ignore that, we won't be just making peace with less than half or with one-third of the Palestinian people. It's that one-third who are not refugees, who will not accept any peace that fragments them or that denies the rights of the refugees.

In a sense, we are all refugees. We have all been alienated and painfully separated from our rights, from our history, from our most basic rights. So what we need is, first of all, a genuine recognition, an admission of guilt and culpability by Israel; the real authentic narrative of the Palestinians to come out, to be acknowledged, to be recognized.

And it is ironic that only when Israeli historians like Benny Morris, Tom Sager, and [U.S.] Finkelstein, and others have the courage to try to set the historical record straight, to explore through the very scholarly work examining the archives, intelligence archives of Israel, the documents of the British Mandate and so on, that the real story began to come out, because it was not being told by the victim but by the oppressor, by the perpetrators of the act. So it began to gain an audience. It's being fought, I know. There are many people who don't want their story to come out. They don't want to tarnish it. They don't want to have reality intrude on the myth and the image and the legend of the heroic creation of the state of Israel.[4] People don't want to face the tremendous pain and suffering, the incredible cost that establishment of the state of Israel involved, particularly with the Palestinian people.

And so once these historians started speaking out, some others, who were also part of the act of commission, who were in the armed Jewish gangs in 1947-48, whether in the Haganah or Stern started speaking out, actually; whether it is the historical guilt or whether it is a recognition that now people can face the truth. But they started speaking out and they started, in a sense, a public confession of their role in the ethnic cleansing of Palestine, which included systematic, brutal, cold-blooded murder, like Tantura, which just finally came out only this year, a few months back, or massacres like those of Deir Yassin, as well and later massacres of Urkasa and many unknown massacres.[5]

Two, there was a systematic attempt at the expulsion of Palestinians through fear and intimidation. There was also a very conscious expulsion where people were herded off, were put in trucks and buses or were made to walk by force of arms, and where they were expelled. There was also a general atmosphere of fear, intimidation, threats of further massacres. The 418 villages that were totally demolished are still a very eloquent expression of this type of ethnic cleansing that has gone without accountability and with total impunity, actually.

And, of course, the worst crime, it seems to me, has been the silence and the denial of the facts and of the history and of the real human narrative and the refusal to assume responsibility. To compound that real injustice was also the subjugation of Palestinian rights to political convenience and political deals. And one thing that we must not do in the peace process is to accept such a distortion, and once again to subjugate Palestinian rights to political convenience or to the politics of power or to strategic alliances.

Israel is not a country above the law and is not a country that should be held by different standards. There are uniform standards that govern the behavior of all civilized nations. They should apply equally across the board. If Israel wants to be a country, a state among states, then it has to abide by these standards. It has to be held responsible, not just for its past sins and crimes, but also for the ongoing, continuing violations that it is involved in. Israel cannot be given a priori dispensation. They cannot wipe the slate clean and say, "Now we will deal with history in another way. The political process is a new process and must not be taken back." Well, for the process to have integrity and legality and credibility and to achieve results, it has to be precisely with these issues, with this narrative, with the Palestinian refugee question, with the unity of the Palestinian people as a people, as a nation, who had a past and therefore should have a future.

The present is extremely painful and difficult. When Israel talks about, legislates a law of return for any Jewish people who happen to be anywhere in the world, to gain instant rights in Palestine and Israel, we are being told that the right of return of the Palestinian refugees, which is not only based on the specific resolution relevant, pertinent to the Palestinian question, whether it is 181, or 194 in particular—which has been annually reaffirmed, actually, has never been denied, 194— but also using universal criteria, universal instruments of human rights, can be disregarded. Along with the Hague regulations, the Third and Fourth Geneva regulations and all the precedents that we have missed and miss, of resolutions, of precedents, of instruments of international humanitarian law that guarantee us those rights.

And yet we are being told to show a positive attitude and to be committed to the peace process. We must not talk about issues which are delicate and sensitive and which might upset the Israelis. Well, reality is much more painful than even describing it. So if the victim cannot speak out and if we cannot deal with these issues, and if we cannot resolve them, there can be no peace. International law is there in order to protect the vulnerable and the helpless. And the Palestinians have always been vulnerable and exposed and helpless. But once we've decided that we do not cherish the role of victim and that we want to sort of make history, take the bull by the horns and change the course of history, we are being told, "You must adopt the narrative of the others. You must abandon or distort your history." We are not going to do that.

Every time we speak out, we get statements, official statements about how this is extremist language and it's against the peace process. A peace process that is not based on international law is no peace process and no instrument of peace. A peace process that does not recognize the essential human component of the human tragedy and does not come to grips with it and attempt to solve it is no peace process. We did not enter negotiations to surrender. We entered negotiations to effect an historical reconciliation. And to do that, the refugee issue, Jerusalem, our land boundaries, our rights, resources, these have to be recognized and these have to be solved on the basis of justice and historical redemption, if you will. Otherwise, if these narratives continue to be excluded, if Palestinian refugees are going to be treated by different standards, if Israel continues to be above the law and immune from accountability, then we certainly don't want such a rogue state as a neighbor.

It is not Iraq or Iran. We believe that the real rogue state in the region is another "I"—Israel. Unless it abides by international law, unless it comes to grips with its own history and unless it takes serious steps to have this legality incorporated in the peace process, not just as recognition of guilt, as I said, but also as a means of rectification, we will not be able to have peace. And anybody who tells you that the Palestinians will be happy with a few reservations here and there that are described as Bantustans or will be happy in an apartheid system or will accept to suffer from collective amnesia suddenly and forget their past and forget their human reality, these people are sadly mistaken. This is precisely the substance of peace. And people who want to make peace have to have the courage to address these issues.

Otherwise, we'll be skirting the issues. We will be dealing with a temporary truce. But then the causes of conflict will remain in place and they will erupt eventually. The peace process is not there to prepare the ground for future conflict. It is not the capitulation of the weak or the exploitation of the weakness of the weak by the strong. It is the vindication of the suffering of the weak in order to overcome it, in order to find genuine solutions, and in order to effect historical reconciliation which will empower the weak and create a situation of human parity based on international legality that would bring about a peace that can lay claim to permanence and justice.

I thank you for coming here today. And I think what Jawdat has said has been more eloquent than anything I can say. But I urge you to keep your ears open, to listen carefully to the individual narrative and to the real history, to the new historians or the post- Zionist historians, if you will, and from those, to glean the necessary lessons and mechanisms to affect a real solution. Thank you very much. (Applause.)

MR. BOYLE: Thank you, Dr. Ashrawi. I've been asked to chair the question-and-answer session. So raise your hand, identify yourself, who you would like to answer the question, and we'll take it from there. Yes.

Q: (Inaudible)—for the neighboring countries and—(inaudible). What is the solution that's going to—how is the situation going to—(inaudible)?

MS. ASHRAWI: Yes. This is really a crucial question, because the refugee question is a key to stability and to peace in the whole region. I've attended several meetings and conferences in Europe, where they talk about, you know, displacement, where they talk about refugees and immigrants or they talk about political asylum. And they say this is going to disturb or upset western demographic standards, western labor issues and so on. And I said one country in Europe maybe has 10,000 refugees and Palestinians who took asylum there. I said what you have is the tip of an iceberg. It's the neighboring countries—in any conflict, the neighboring countries are those who suffer and those who have to accept massive demographic pressure, shifts and distortions in their own country. Now, the three major countries, of course, neighboring countries that took in Palestinian refugees were Jordan, Syria and Lebanon, of course. The conditions of the Palestinian refugees in these areas are not the same.

In Lebanon, and it is no secret, the plight of the Palestinians is particularly tragic because of internal Lebanese problems, balances, demographic, sectarian, whatever balances. The Palestinian refugees have been sort of living in a time warp with a total denial of their human and civil rights.[6]   And their suffering has been compounded. They're not recognized as human beings with full rights, and they have been treated as a political problem, as a threat to a demographic balance, but without really addressing the real human and political issue. Now we hear talk openly that—and, of course, there are movements in Lebanon and elsewhere saying that they are against absorption of Palestinian refugees. Nobody is calling for the absorption of Palestinian refugees in their host countries. We are calling for respect for their human and civil rights in their host countries, to be treated as human beings, until we solve the question on a legal and political basis, number one.

Number two, the right of return should be affirmed. It's not what we are against. Of course people don't want to be absorbed; otherwise they would have been absorbed. They have a right to their own identity, to their own homes, to repatriation and to restitution of their rights, which is why I particularly like the name of CPRR. And the host countries cannot, under the heat of the moment, in the course of the peace process, start trying to make individual deals to solve the question of the refugee population in their own countries. What is needed first is a unified Arab position on the right of return. We need coordination and a unified strategy with the Arabs on negotiating the right of return.

Three, the Palestinian leadership, the PLO, is the only body empowered to negotiate on behalf of the Palestinians and to represent all the Palestinians, including the refugees. And the refugees have to be part of this negotiation and the solution. They cannot be excluded. They are not pawns. Now, we understand that there are political problems and difficulties in different countries, but that doesn't mean that the Palestinian refugees are games and it doesn't mean that bilateral agreements with Israel, with any host country—be it Jordan, be it Syria, be it Lebanon—would be acceptable to us. The refugee question has to be solved in total as a central issue of solving the Palestinian question based on the implementation of international law, and in particular U.N. Resolution 194, and then there will be a real solution.

But no single country can negotiate the nationality, the plight, the residency and the rights of the refugees it hosts. And until we do that, we urge all host countries to treat the Palestinian refugees with the dignity, the consideration, and the legal rights and human rights that they deserve. That's why it's become very, very urgent. This fragmentation of the Arab position will be to the detriment of everybody. And I believe it's the Palestinians who will have to take the initiative, but we have to have a receptive Arab world in order to coordinate that.

We understood that Jordan, for example—there were talks about compensation of Jordan for hosting refugees, and there were talks about future compensation for Jordan for absorbing refugees or integrating the Palestinians in Jordan. Now, such talk at this time would be extremely dangerous. This cannot be done, as I said, separately. The refugees are not just populations in each country. They are a serious not just demographic but political issue, and they affect directly the stability of the region and the security of the whole region, because they're not going to disappear. And if there is an abstract decision taken by big powers that the refugees will be absorbed wherever they were, it doesn't mean that that decision can be resolved—or can be implemented, sorry. And it doesn't mean that the Palestinian refugees will accept it. And I cannot separate the Palestinian refugees from the rest of the Palestinians who are not refugees. Again, as they are two-thirds of the Palestinian people, you have a total consensus among the Palestinians that this is the cause of the Palestinian condition.

Q: My name is Khalid Jhashan. I'm with N-triple-A-ADC. I'd like to commend CPRR for undertaking this worthy campaign that fills a huge vacuum in the continuing struggle of the Palestinians to achieve justice and lasting peace. My question is actually addressed to Francis with regards to the legal background of this issue. You mentioned two precedents with regard to this case. You forgot to mention possibly a third one. Would you care to comment on the recent proactive role that the U.S. administration has taken in securing compensation for victims of the Holocaust and making several countries in Europe pay for their sins of the past, if you will? Is this applicable? Is this also a third kind of precedent that might be applicable to the case of the Palestinians?

MR. BOYLE: It is a precedent, yes, although in the case of the Palestinians, of course, we want them all to go home, whereas many of these Jewish refugees from the Nazi Holocaust have decided voluntarily to settle in other countries. And I can certainly understand why Jewish refugees from the Nazi Holocaust would not want to go back to Germany or Austria or whatever. But the critical point to keep in mind under Resolution 194, this is an individual right that each Palestinian refugee has. Do they want to go back to their homes or, like the Jewish refugees from the Nazi Holocaust, do they want to stay where they are and accept reparations for the property and other things that have been taken from them? So it is a precedent in the sense of the either/or of Resolution 194, yes.

Q: The arguments of time so many times are thrown back in our faces when we discuss the aspects of return of refugees. How do you deal with it?

MS. ASHRAWI: Well, since, by international law—and I'm sure Francis can answer that better—war crimes are not subject to—what do they call it when—

MR. BOYLE: Statute of limitations.

MS. ASHRAWI: Yes, statute of limitations. And I believe what happened to Palestinians is a form of ethnic cleansing, which is a war crime par excellence. And the right of Palestinian refugees has never been relinquished in any way or modified, because 194 has been affirmed annually in the U.N. by member states, and then it has become even more pressing.

So the fact that suffering has been extended over such a long period of time doesn't mean that now we will modify or relinquish those rights that they have because they've suffered longer than other refugees. It's the fault of the international community that Israel was not made to comply with the law, was not made to implement U.N. resolutions. But to make the Palestinians pay the price again because Israel did not comply would be another serious mistake. And I believe the question of time can be answered not just in legal terms and in human rights terms, but also can be answered in terms of political necessity if there is to be peace.

The Palestinians, who have long been waiting for their right to return to their homes, should have that right not just acknowledged, but should be made possible to exercise. Now, if you want to start discussing the implementation, if your home has been demolished, your village razed and obliterated from existence and so on, it doesn't mean that you don't want to go back. You may want to go back, but you will also have to have compensation and you will have to be repatriated and compensated for your loss for the use of your land that others have used, for the disruption in your life, as well as for the property itself. So it's not an impossible issue. And I think, using the yardstick that this is sensitive for Israel or that this will upset the demographic balance in Israel or this will not be in conformity with Zionism, we as Palestinians do not view our job to safeguard Zionism. It is our job to safeguard our rights.

Q: (Off mike.)

MS. ASHRAWI: Yes. Well, I have with me here the documents pertaining to the refugee question, both in negotiating talks and strategic documents from the Palestinian negotiation affairs department. And it's not the Palestinian Authority that's negotiating; it's the PLO that is negotiating. There is a consensus among all Palestinians, which is an issue not subject to manipulation by a government, to say, "I have the right or I have been given the mandate to undermine or modify the rights of Palestinian refugees." Therefore, this consensus exists at the public level, at the popular level, at the official level.

I was telling friends here that we have meetings almost every day, at least once a week, public meetings, discussions, seminars, specialized talks, expert papers and so on, on permanent status issues, and in particular on the refugees. **And there is a strong drive and will among the people that this issue has to be resolved by implementing 194 and that nobody has the right to abandon 194 or to find alternative solutions. And I think the PLO is quite aware that this is one area that we cannot in any way give concessions or abandon rights and stay in power as a representative of the Palestinian people as a whole, because if you have the majority of the people who are sending you a very clear message and who have taken a very clear, decisive, firm stance on this issue, your legitimacy, your legality would be in serious doubt if you stopped representing those people.**

So the legality and the legitimacy of any representative authority has to come from the people, and this is the people's position. And no leadership, PLO or otherwise, can change that. And I believe firmly, from all the people I've talked to—and I am in touch daily with them—that there is no inclination to attempt to sell short the Palestinian right of return. [Emphasis supplied.]

MR. BOYLE: I do want to emphasize for the news media the one point Dr. Ashrawi made. The Palestinian Authority does not have any legal right to represent the Palestinian people as a whole for any reason whatsoever. That authority is in the hands of the Palestine Liberation Organization, which has an executive committee that currently serves as the provisional government of the state of Palestine. The state of Palestine today now has a de jure diplomatic recognition by about 127 or 128 states. That's more than have diplomatic recognition, the last time I looked, with Israel. That's de jure diplomatic recognition as a state. They also now have, the state of Palestine, de facto membership at the United Nations Organization. We would have de jure U.N. membership at the United Nations Organization if not for the clearly illegal threat of a veto by the United States government. We have de facto recognition as a state by most of Europe. And the only thing that has kept Europe from recognizing the Palestinian state de jure has been massive pressure applied by the United States government.

Now, last spring the European Union adopted a position that they are prepared to give de jure recognition to the Palestinian state within a year. And I believe that this will come to pass. And certainly I believe that Palestine will be admitted de jure to the United Nations Organization. It's only fair under Resolution 181—one state for the Jewish people, one state for the Palestinian people, U.N. membership for Israel, U.N. membership for Palestine. It is inevitable. It will happen. The longer it takes, the more difficult negotiating peace will be. But again, the critical point to keep in mind is that the Palestinian Authority does not have the right to negotiate on behalf of the Palestinian people. That's in the PLO, its executive committee. And the PLO represents all the Palestinian people, not just those living in occupied Palestine. Another question, please. Yes.

Q: (Off mike.) Is peace really possible between Israelis and Palestinians?

MR. BOYLE: All I can say is this to the Israeli people and their supporters here in the United States. It was my job, as the legal adviser to the Palestinian delegation to the Middle East peace negotiations—my instructions were to figure out a way to do this in good faith. My client is the Palestinian people, all of them. But, of course, in doing this, I had to take into account the reasonable good-faith expectations of the Israeli people for peace with justice. I can assure you the will is there on the part of the Palestinian people and the Palestinian leadership for peace with justice. But there will be no peace if the United States and the Israeli government attempt to impose a Bantustan on the Palestinian people. It will not happen.

Hanan, why don't you make the final conclusion? We're about out of time.

MS. ASHRAWI: Okay. To respond to that question, I think the PLO has always been a sort of national representative body, because in a sense it represented Palestinians everywhere, not just in one location. The Palestinian National Authority represents the Palestinians on the West Bank and Gaza, where we had direct elections. But it emerged from the interim phase agreements. So we say that the PNA is temporary for part of the people on part of the land for some of the time, until we end up with statehood. And now what we have to do is really working on embodying statehood in Palestine, and that's another issue which takes a long time to respond. And I think this year, we will see the Palestinian state officially sort of being declared and accepted. The important thing is to make sure that we have the constitution and the institutions of state and the separation of powers and the democratic principles implemented, as well as the sovereignty over all of the territories occupied in '67. That's the real question, because Israel wants to dictate its own terms on what the Palestinian state should be, its territorial domain, as well as the degree of sovereignty or control.

As far as Israeli public opinion is concerned, of course you don't have a consensus and of course you have many opinions. And I think it's split down the middle. There are many anti-peace forces in Israel. There are extreme fundamentalist elements in Israel who think that they have the power of life and death over the Palestinians and should continue to do that. It's these forces who assassinated Rabin, these forces who assassinated many others, the many massacres of Palestinians killed daily by people who don't react to them with the sort of tragic dimension that accompanies the killing of an Israeli because of this double-standard assessment of human life, and, of course, the desensitization and inurement when it comes to Palestinian life and rights.

What has to be done is to form a force for peace in Israel by having a public discourse and strategy and policy that would validate peace, that would not, on the one hand, maintain the mentality of the occupier and the racist mentality of control and domination, and at the same time claim that they want to make peace and then try to distort the peace process to fit conditions of occupation or conditions of control. This isn't going to happen. So while we have contributed to the formation of an Israeli public opinion towards a peace strategy or a peace movement and we have been in dialogue for a long time, at the same time there is a tremendous gap between the decision-making, on the one hand, and public opinion on the other. And there are serious internal fragmentations within Israeli public opinion. To influence public opinion, you have to have the courage and the openness to clearly state, as an Israeli leadership, what is needed to make peace. You cannot, as they say, have your cake and eat it, too. You have to state clearly that all territory occupied in '67 has to be restored to its owners, that the substantive issues on permanent status agenda have to be resolved on the basis of legality, foremost among which is the right of return, and you have to be truthful with your constituency. You cannot mislead them into peace. And that is one of the serious shortcomings of the Israeli leadership. There is a crisis in leadership, and generally we find that both parties in Israeli, both main parties—there are many other parties—generally are competing on the terrain of extremism rather than on the language of peace. Thank you very much. (Applause.)

A New Direction For The Palestinian People
by Francis A. Boyle
Professor of International Law
Legal Advisor to the Palestinian Delegation to the Middle East
Peace Negotiations (1991-93)

When the Oslo Document was originally presented by the Israeli government to the Palestinian Delegation to the Middle East Peace Negotiations in the Fall of 1992, it was rejected by the Delegation because it obviously constituted less than a Bantustan. This document carried out Menachem Begin's disingenuous misinterpretation of the Camp David Accords--expressly rejected by U.S. President Jimmy Carter—which was that all they called for was a form of non-territorial autonomy: i.e., autonomy for the Palestinian people but not for their land as well.

Soon thereafter, unbeknownst to the Palestinian Delegation in Washington and to almost everyone else, the Israeli government opened up a secret channel of negotiations with PLO in Norway. There the Israeli government re-presented the document that had already been rejected by the Palestinian Delegation in Washington, D.C. It was this document, with very minor modifications, that was later signed at the White House on 13 September 1993.

Before the signing ceremony, I commented to a high level official of the Palestine Liberation Organization: "This document is like a straightjacket. It will be very difficult to negotiate your way out of it." This PLO official agreed with my assessment and responded: "Yes, you are right. It will depend upon our negotiating skill."

Of course I have great respect for Palestinian negotiators.

They have done the best they can, negotiating in good faith with an Israeli government that has been invariably backed up by the United States. But there has never been any good faith on the part of the Israeli government either before, during, or after Oslo. Ditto for the United States.

Even if Oslo had succeeded, it would have resulted in the imposition of a Bantustan upon the Palestinian People rather than implementing their true right to self-determination in a state of their own. But Oslo has run its course! Therefore, it is my purpose here today to chart a **New Direction** for the Palestinian People to consider:

An Agenda for an international legal response:

1. We must immediately move for the de facto suspension of Israel throughout the entirety of the United Nations System, including the General Assembly and all U.N. subsidiary organs and bodies. We must do to Israel what the U.N. General Assembly has done to the genocidal Yugoslavia and to the criminal apartheid regime in South Africa! The legal basis for the de facto suspension of Israel at the U.N. is quite simple:

As a condition for its admission to the United Nations Organization, Israel formally agreed to accept General Assembly Resolution 181 (II) (1947) (partition/Jerusalem trusteeship) and General Assembly Resolution 194 (III) (1948) (Palestinian right of return), inter alia. Nevertheless, the government of Israel has expressly repudiated both Resolution 181 (II) and Resolution 194 (III). Therefore, Israel has violated its conditions for admission to U.N. membership and thus must be suspended on a de facto basis from any participation throughout the entire United Nations System.

2. Any further negotiations with Israel must be conducted on the basis of Resolution 181 (II) and its borders; Resolution 194 (III); subsequent General Assembly resolutions and Security Council resolutions; the Third and Fourth Geneva Conventions of 1949; the 1907 Hague Regulations; and other relevant principles of public international law.

3. We must abandon the fiction and the fraud that the United States government is an "honest broker." The United States government has never been an honest broker from well before the very outset of these negotiations in 1991. Rather, the United States has invariably sided with Israel against the Palestinians. We need to establish some type of international organizational framework to sponsor these negotiations where the Palestinian negotiators will not be subjected to the continual bullying, threats, harassment, intimidation and outright

lies perpetrated by the United States government—perhaps the U.N. Trusteeship Council, which is independent of both the U.N. General Assembly and the Security Council.

4. We must move to have the U.N. General Assembly impose economic, diplomatic, and travel sanctions upon Israel pursuant to the terms of the Uniting for Peace Resolution (1950), whose Emergency Special Session on Palestine is now in recess.

5. The Provisional Government of the State of Palestine must sue Israel before the International Court of Justice in The Hague for inflicting acts of genocide against the Palestinian People in violation of the 1948 Genocide Convention!

6. The United Nations General Assembly must immediately establish an International Criminal Tribunal for Israel (ICTI) as a "subsidiary organ" under U.N. Charter Article 22. The ICTI would be organized along the lines of the International Criminal Tribunal for Yugoslavia (ICTY), which was established by the Security Council. The purpose of the ICTI would be to investigate and prosecute Israeli war crimes, crimes against humanity, and genocide against the Peoples of Lebanon and Palestine—just as the ICTY did for the victims of international crimes committed by Yugoslavia and the Milosevic Regime throughout the Balkans.

The establishment of the ICTI would provide some small degree of justice to the victims of Israeli war crimes, crimes against humanity, and genocide against the Peoples of Lebanon and Palestine—just as the ICTY has done in the Balkans. Furthermore, the establishment of the ICTI by the U.N. General Assembly would serve as a deterrent effect upon Israeli leaders such as the Prime Minister, Foreign Minister, Defense Minister, Chief of Staff, and Israel's other top generals that they will be prosecuted for their further infliction of international crimes upon the Palestinians and the Lebanese.

Without such a deterrent, Israel might be emboldened to attack Syria with the full support of America's Neo-Conservative operatives who have always viewed Syria as "low-hanging fruit" ready to be taken out by means of their joint aggression. If Israel attacks Syria as it did when it invaded Lebanon in 1982, Iran has vowed to come to Syria's defense. And of course Israel and United States government very much want a pretext to attack Iran. This scenario could readily degenerate into World War III. For the U.N. General Assembly to establish the ICTI could stop the further development of this momentum towards a regional if not global catastrophe.

These six steps taken in conjunction with each other should

be enough to enable the Palestinian People to obtain restitution, reparations, and the return to their homes and lands--Inshallah! By contrast, if the Oslo process is continued, it will inevitably result in the imposition of a Bantustan upon the Palestinian People living in occupied Palestine, as well as the final dispossession and disenfranchisement and displacement of all Palestinian People living in the Diaspora. Consequently, I call upon all Palestinian People living everywhere in the world to unite behind this **New Direction** that I have sketched out here today.

NOTE: Professor Boyle's call for an International Criminal Tribunal for Israel is now being circulated by member states of the U.N. General Assembly. On January 4, 2009, Nobel Peace Prize Laureate Mairead Maguire of Ireland wrote to the U.N. Secretary General, Ban Ki-Moon and Father Miguel D'Escoto President of the United Nations General Assembly, adding her voice to the many calls from international jurists, human rights organizations, and individuals, for the U.N. General Assembly to establish an International Criminal Tribunal for Israel in view of the ongoing Israeli atrocities against the People of Palestine, especially in Gaza.

NOTES

1   Janine Zacharia, *Refugee Issue Threatens Israel's U.N. Standing,* Jerusalem Post, March 5, 2000.

2   Universal Declaration of Human Rights, Article 13(2) (1948): "Everyone has the right to leave any country, including his own, and to return to his country."

3   *See* Hanan Ashrawi, This Side of Peace (1995).

4   *See, e.g.,* Paul Findley, Deliberate Deceptions: Facing the FACTS about the U.S.-Israeli Relationship (1993).

5   *See* Issa Nakhleh, 1 & 2 Encyclopedia of the Palestine Problem (1991).

6   *See* Franklin Lamb, *Lebanon: No Substantive Change for Palestinians,* Anti-imperialist Camp, Aug. 22, 2010 and *Chickenfeed for the Soul,* Counterpunch.org, Aug. 18, 2010.

Chapter Two

The Palestinian Right of Return
with Dr. Haidar Abdul Shafi

Council for Palestinian Restitution and Repatriation
Date: Thu, 20 Apr 2000
Title: CPRR Press Release 20/4/2000
MEDIA ADVISORY

Former Chief Palestinian Negotiator to Issue Warning to Israel About Right of Return for Palestinian Refugees

In the face of Israeli demands that Palestinian refugees not be allowed to return under any peace agreement, elder Palestinian statesman and former head of the Palestinian negotiating team to the Madrid and Washington talks, Dr. Haidar Abdul Shafi will issue a stern warning to the Israeli government regarding the Palestinian right of return and restitution.

In addition, Francis Boyle, Professor of International Law at the University of Illinois, will discuss legal alternatives for the Palestinian people relating to the Oslo Accords and building on precedents set by the international community's intervention on behalf of Kosovar refugees. As far as the Palestinian people are concerned, the rights to return and restitution are the most central issues in the current peace negotiations between the Palestinian Authority and Israel.

Both Dr. Abdul Shafi and Professor Boyle are board members of the newly-formed Council on Palestinian Restitution and Repatriation (CPRR). Dr. Abdul Shafi is one of the most respected personalities in Palestinian politics and is considered to be the unofficial spokesperson for the Palestinian people. Professor Boyle served as the legal advisor for the Palestinian delegation to the Middle East negotiations from 1991 to 1993.

Dr. Abdul Shafi and Professor Boyle are also available for a limited number of interviews. CPRR was created in response to growing Palestinian concerns that the outcome of final status negotiations will not resolve the refugee crisis – a crisis which has spanned 52 years. CPRR provides legal aid to Palestinians in achieving their rights and has, since its creation in December, gathered tens of thousands of signatures for its petition affirming these rights.

News Briefing of the
Council for Palestinian Restitution and Repatriation
News Release

For immediate release: April 21, 2000

CALLS FOR PALESTINIAN RIGHT OF RETURN

WASHINGTON--Today the former head of the Palestinian negotiating team asserted the right of Palestinian refugees to return to their homes. Dr. Haidar Abdul Shafi, who led the Palestinian delegation to the Madrid and Washington talks, said that Palestinians "evicted out by terrorism and force" should be allowed back to their homes. "This is a matter that should go to the conscience of the world--and the democratic world especially." Saying that "the refugee issue is the heart and the core of the problem," Abdul Shafi, a physician from Gaza and widely-respected Palestinian leader, called on the Palestinian Authority to include "the issue of the Palestinian refugees on the basis of Resolution 194" in the negotiations. Abdul Shafi was joined by Francis Boyle, Professor of International Law at the University of Illinois, who served as legal advisor to the Palestinian delegation. He also cited UN Security Council Resolution 194, passed in 1948 and calling for the return of the refugees at the "earliest practicable date."

In response to a question, Abdul Shafi replied that the current Palestinian leadership "will disqualify itself" if it were to sign away the right to return. Buttressing his case for the right of Palestinians to return to their homes, Boyle cited U.S. policy favoring family reunification of Soviet Jews and compensation for losses resulting from the Nazi Holocaust. He also noted that the Universal Declaration of Human Rights asserts "everyone has the right to return to his country." Boyle, who provided legal assistance to the Bosnians and Kosovar Albanians, also cited the precedent of Kosovar refugees to return to their homes in the aftermath of the NATO bombing of Yugoslavia. "The Palestinians should have the same right to go back to their homes." Citing Yugoslavia and apartheid South Africa as examples, Boyle warned that "if Israel refuses to implement resolution 194, it will jeopardize its membership in the United Nations" and risk various sanctions. Boyle called the current circumstance "a remarkable opportunity for peace in the Middle

East--if the U.S. and Israel show a commitment to international law."

Palestinians are the largest refugee population in the world, many continue to live in refugee camps in Lebanon, Syria and the occupied territories. Approximately 750,000 were driven from their homes in 1948. Remarks were made at a news conference organized by CPRR.

News Briefing of Council for Palestinian Restitution and Repatriation
Washington, D.C.
April 21, 2000

MR. SHAFI: Thank you and good morning, ladies and gentlemen.

I speak to you on behalf of the Palestinian Council for the Restitution and Repatriation of the Palestinian Refugees. I shall limit my talk to this issue, specifically, to the issue of the rights of the Palestinian refugees. Now, as the peace negotiations have reached the stage of discussing the framework of the final negotiations of the peace process, we think that the Palestine Authority should include in this framework the issue of the Palestinian refugees, on the basis of Resolution 194. We think very strongly that this is very necessary. The refugee issue is the heart and the core of the peace problem, and we call on our Authority to do that in all seriousness and sincerity.

Now, we know very well that the Palestinian Authority is going to be pressured very strongly, basically I think by the United States government and by Israel and maybe by other parties, not to do that, not to put the refugee issue on the agenda of the framework for the final negotiations. And I hope that the Palestinian Authority would stand firm on its responsibility of the necessity of having the refugee issue, in the context of Resolution 194, on the final-stage negotiations. I think, as you can imagine, the—trying to relegate—I mean, they will press that the issue should not be put on the agenda of the final status negotiations, but they would want to relegate it to the future. And that, of course, will deprive the peace negotiations from any real content and any seriousness and, of course, this will be very detrimental and it will be a death blow to the peace negotiations as such. So really we cannot overemphasize this issue and, as I said, we expect that our Authority will do that in seriousness and strength. That's all I need to say about this issue.

We have received tens of thousands of signatures from Palestinian refugees all over the Middle East and in the occupied territories affirming their right to repatriation and restitution, and we feel the responsibility and obligation as the Council, for the cause of the refugees and restitution and the repatriation, to emphasize this matter very much and to voice this call to our Authority first, to be aware of the seriousness of the matter, and also to all the parties who are involved in peace, especially the United States government and the world democracies in general. Thank you very much.

MR. BOYLE: Thank you, Dr. Abdul Shafi. I hope everyone in this room understands that Dr. Abdul Shafi came all the way from Gaza just to be here and to make it perfectly clear to the United States government and to Israel that there will be no peace unless Resolution 194 is carried out. Israel accepted Resolution 194 as a condition for its membership in the United Nations Organization: the Palestinian Right of Return. And here, let me quote this language. Quote: "Resolves that the refugees wishing to return to their homes and live at peace with their neighbors should be permitted to do so at the earliest practicable date and that compensation should be paid for the property of those choosing not to return and for loss of or damage to property which, under principles of international law or in equity, should be made good by the governments or authorities responsible." Unquote.

Now, for years here in the United States we heard an enormous amount about the right of family reunification for Soviet Jews, and the United States government was at the forefront of that battle. Likewise today, we heard President Clinton say that he was in favor of family reunification for Elian Gonzalez and his father, Juan. Well, there are about 5 million Palestinian refugees who need to be relocated, reunified, with their families, with their homes, and with their lands.

And here, let me quote from the Universal Declaration of Human Rights, which, by the way, the United States government invoked to support reunification of Soviet Jews and the United States government has invoked all over the world in support of family reunification. Quote: "Everyone has the right... to return to his country."[1] Unquote. And the United States government has consistently taken the position that this is a right of customary international law.

Just recently, we have two instances where the United States government has stood up for the rights of refugees to return to their homes. In the Dayton Agreement for Bosnia, drafted by the State

Department, supervised by Richard Holbrooke, it says quite clearly that the Bosnian refugees have the right to return to their homes. The same principle must be applied to the Palestinian refugees.

Just recently, a year ago, NATO intervened in Kosovo and went to war with Serbia to guarantee the right of the Kosovar Albanian refugees, to return to their homes. This process is now going on under the direct supervision of NATO, the European Union, the United Nations and the United States. The same must be done for the Palestinian refugees.

Let me make it quite clear that if Israel refuses to implement Resolution 194, it will jeopardize its membership in the United Nations Organization. As I said, as a condition for its admission to the U.N., Israel formally agreed to accept Resolution 194 of 1948, and General Assembly Resolution 181 of 1947, demanding the partition of the Palestine Mandate into two states—a Jewish state and an Arab state; and an international trusteeship for Jerusalem.[2]   If Israel continues to refuse to recognize and implement Resolution 194 and Resolution 181, it can lead to the de facto suspension of Israel from the United Nations Organization.[3] This is exactly what has been done to, what at that point in time was a criminal apartheid regime in South Africa, and also to the government of the genocidal Yugoslavia, that still today does not participate in the activities of the United Nations Organization.

Second, if Israel continues to refuse to implement Resolutions 194 and 181—and, by the way, Prime Minister Barak has rejected both Resolutions publicly—the provisional government of the state of Palestine can move to have the United Nations General Assembly adopt comprehensive economic, diplomatic and travel sanctions against Israel pursuant to the terms of the Uniting for Peace Resolution of 1950. Palestine has already invoked the Uniting for Peace Resolution successfully against Israel in the General Assembly. Right now, the General Assembly's emergency special session on Palestine is in recess, but it can be recalled at any time.[4]

Third, any further negotiations with Israel must be conducted on the basis of Resolution 181 and its borders; Resolution 194; subsequent General Assembly resolutions and Security Council resolutions; the Third and Fourth Geneva Conventions of 1949; the 1907 Hague Regulations; and other relevant principles of public international law. So far, the Israeli government has not negotiated in good faith in accordance with these basic principles of international law and, I regret to report, the United States government has supported Israel in its defiance of basic terms of international law and the terms of reference for these negotiations.

There is a remarkable opportunity here for peace in the Middle East, but this is going to require that the United States government and the Israeli government adhere to these basic principles of international law that I have outlined for you here today. If Israel and the United States do not adhere to these principles, I regret to say I don't believe there will be a durable peace in the Middle East.

Thank you.

I've now been asked to chair the question and answer session. Please identify yourself and your affiliation and whether you wish your question to go to Dr. Abdul Shafi or myself.
(Pause.)

As I say to my students: It's all so clear, there are no questions?

(Laughter.)

Yes?

Q: Yes. Dr. Abdul Shafi, do you have contacts with some of the outside Palestinian refugees in Jordan, Syria and in the West Bank, for that matter, and particularly those in Lebanon? And what impact does this idea of return and restitution and increasing compensation have on your relationship with those refugees still in the camps?

MR. SHAFI: It certainly has a very great impact on all Palestinians, not on me alone. This is a matter of right. And all of us know the history of this refugee question; how they were forced out of their habitat by terror and violence and all this. And so they are very much attached to this Resolution 194, and I think it is in their own right to claim this legally and from all points of view, and we certainly stand in support of them on this. And I hope that our Authority will prove its standing to the occasion.

Q: Actually, I have two questions, first of all, regarding the Palestinian Authority itself. Have they started taking measures to accommodate the refugees if they come back, because, you know, they can take them back anytime. Or are they limited to the numbers by Israel?

MR. SHAFI: Nobody, as you probably don't know—nobody is

repatriated except by an Israeli permission. Nobody is allowed to come to the Palestinian territory except through an Israeli permission. So the returnees are very limited, and this is all together under the discretion of Israel.

Q: And the other part of the question is regarding Israel itself. One time I interviewed an Israeli official, and I raised this question with him, and he said this means—the return of the Palestinian refugees means the death of Israel, so nobody in his mind would accept that, because this actually would imbalance the demographical...

MR. SHAFI: It need not be so. Initially the Zionist movement claimed all of Palestine, and they knew that Palestine had its own indigenous people, and they decided that their program cannot be implemented except by force, and they continue to claim all Palestine. But in reality, there is a place for the refugees. Now, a Palestinian researcher, Abu Sittah, recently made a detailed study about whether there is room for repatriation or not, and he made it very evident there is plenty of room for repatriation.[5] And anyhow, Israel cannot claim the land for itself alone and deprive indigenous people of their right to self-determination.

Q: Correct me if I'm wrong. Does the PNA have the right to negotiate about the Palestinian people right of return, or is the right of the PLO to do that, as a representative of the Palestinian people?

MR. SHAFI: Well, the negotiating—the present negotiating delegation negotiates in the name of the Palestinian people.

Q: But the PLO or the PNA has the right to negotiate?

MR. SHAFI: Well, I'm sorry that this matter is blurred, and it should not be. And it's the responsibility of the Palestinian leadership to make this very clear. I mean, for the short term, it looked as though the PLO is marginalized, and this is wrong. But actually, there is no conflict. The Palestinian—the PNA is supposed to implement the rulings of the PLO.

Q: (Off mike)—do you have any indications whether the negotiators will insist – the Palestinian—on dealing with this matter in the final settlement by the 13th of September? Many fear that an ambiguous language will be used to cover, to deal with this issue, and it will be pushed further. I mean, what are indications from talking to various. . .

MR. SHAFI: That's exactly why we are here, as the Council for restitution, repatriation of the refugees, we are insisting upon. That's why we affirm in this peace conference, we call on the Palestinian Authority to insist on having the question of the refugees according to Resolution 194 to be on the agenda of the framework of the final negotiations.

Yes, ma'am?

Q: Recognizing the validity of their claims, there can be really no—if you look at it legalistically or humanistically, there can be no questioning of it. But in terms of practical negotiation, there has to be a question of it by the Israelis, who as someone has suggested, are immediately going to say, "It destroys the nature of our state"—at least the nature of their state because they wanted and they proclaimed a Zionist Jewish state. And if repatriation occurs, there would be more Arabs than there would be Jews, inside even the pre-1967 borders. Has anyone proposed any way of dealing with this problem politically, so that the Jewish state could feel that it still existed as a national, cultural, political group, as well as offering the same statehood to the Palestinian entity? Are there any practical solutions to this?

MR. SHAFI: Yes, certainly, there could be practical solutions. And there is enough room; I mean it's a matter if Israel claimed all Palestinian territory or if she makes provision for the rights of the Palestinian people; I mean, if she insists on separation. There is talk about a binational state, where Jews and Palestinians live together in equity. But if they insist on separation, then there should be room provided for the Palestinians, and that territory should not all be taken to the Jewish side.

After all, I think—I am sure all of you are aware that, initially, the demographic ratio in Palestine, at the time of the start of the British Mandate, was --Palestinians to Jews—was 11:1. And that was violated very crucially by the British bringing in immigrants against the existence of the Palestinians. So in a span of 25 years, this demographic ratio moved from 11:1 to 2:1, and that was a great violation of the right of the Palestinians to self-determination.

Anyhow, I would want to say at least that Palestinians have exhibited their desire to live peacefully. And as a matter of fact, in the past in the many generations, there was viable co-existence between

Jews and Palestinians in Palestine until this was destroyed by the advent of Zionism.

Now, let me give you just one example about the position of the Palestinian people now in the occupied territories. You know, when the Palestine National Council agreed to go to Madrid, this was not a unanimous decision; it was a majority decision. That means there were opposition parties. So these opposition parties, on the eve of Madrid, they called on the people in the occupied territories to demonstrate against Madrid. Now, what the people did—they did demonstrate in support of Madrid the next day—means that the people who are there, they want peace, but they want peace and equity and justice.

Yes?

Q: Is your presence here an indication of dissension, of differences of opinions within the ranks of the Palestinians' will to negotiate a peaceful settlement?

MR. SHAFI: Well, I don't negate the existence of differences of opinion among Palestinians about what's going on. But here I am not coming with the purpose of dissension, I am just—we are just calling on a very important matter pertaining to the peace process and to the outcome of the peace process, and that it should address in seriousness the issue of the refugees. So we are just calling on the Palestinian Authority, which is engaged in the negotiations, that it should insist that this matter should be on the agenda of the final stage negotiations. That's our purpose.

Q: Have you met with the Palestinian Authority prior to coming here? And do you plan to meet some American officials here?

MR. SHAFI: No, I am not planning to meet any American officials. And I could meet the Palestinian Authority any time I ask for, and why I am in contact.

Q: What do you think would happen in the refugee camps if President Arafat did sign away the right of return, or agree to the return of just a token number of Palestinians?

MR. SHAFI: *I dare say that if the—if our Authority yields on pressures about this issue, it will disqualify itself, I'm sorry to say so. The matter is so serious that it cannot pass by very easily.* [Emphasis supplied.]

Q: I have a question for Mr. Boyle.

Q: It's always known if there is any agreement between Israel and Palestinians or Syrians or whatever, it's always the American taxpayer pays something there. So how do you foresee America's financial involvement in this refugee issue, if there is any solution to it?

MR. BOYLE: Well, my main concern is that you'll have a paper document that won't mean anything; that there will be a document that says: "Oh yes, the Palestinians have a right of return or compensation." Notice it's either/or. But I want to point out; it is their choice as a basic human right. It simply cannot be sold out by anyone purporting to represent them, but it is their choice.

Well, my main concern then would be setting up a fund in name only on paper that is not really funded, or that they call for voluntary contributions alone. Unfortunately, this is what Richard Holbrooke did to the Bosnians: They called for setting up a fund, but it was never funded, and they called for voluntary contributions. Those have been few and far between. So my concern is that there will be some type of paper document recognizing the right, making some titular gesture to this, but when push comes to shove, we will see a very small number of Palestinians actually returning to their homes. And we have to remember here, there are also large numbers of Palestinian refugees living in the West Bank and Gaza in refugee camps, and this right to return also applies to them going back to what is Israel today.

Now, I also want to note one other point for the record. Back in the peace negotiations in 1991, Secretary of State James Baker instructed his press spokesperson at that time, Margaret Tutwiler, to publicly raise the issue of 194, and that issue was publicly raised by Baker and Tutwiler during the course of the negotiations. I was there at the Grand Hotel when this issue came up in public. So it seems to me what we need from the Clinton administration is a recognition of the requirements here for a just peace, and that means the right of return in accordance with the wishes of the Palestinians; it means a genuine independent Palestinian state, not a Bantustan model that is currently being proposed by the United States and Israel; and also some type of shared arrangement for Jerusalem so that Jerusalem can become the capital of both states – a Palestinian state and an Israeli state. And then at that point, the U.S. Embassy could move to Jerusalem and be accredited simultaneously to both states. I think this can be done if there is good faith on the part of the United States and Israel. But so far, I don't believe that is the direction that these negotiations seem to be moving.

MR. SHAFI: I just want to comment further on this matter. You see the refugee problem didn't come about spontaneously. This was premeditated and planned for a long time. Zionist deliberations about moving Palestinians out of Palestine started, actually, before the beginning of the last half of the 20th century, and they were very much in vogue during the '30s. And the Israeli claim that the Palestinians left their homes voluntarily and all this, it's a farce. They were evicted out by terrorism and force and everything like this. [6]

Now, this went into the context of the main Israeli strategy, Zionist strategy, of facing the world with facts on the ground, and this is one of the most painful and serious tactics that Israel has done in this respect, to face the world with fait accompli, and now they face the world with fait accompli around Jerusalem, while they have made changes in the physical character of Jerusalem. But this pertains to humans, so how we can neglect this? I think this is a matter that should go to the conscience of the world, of the democratic world, especially, that this matter could not pass by, that Israelis can get away with a fait accompli that pertains to the lives of people. And so I think this is really a very, very serious matter. It should be very serious, not only for the Palestinians, but for the conscience of the world and the democratic world, especially.

Q: Then, how could you overcome the problem of Israel at this time changing the status of the ownership of some properties over there? Like, most of the properties are listed under absentees' properties, but now they are giving, changing, the numbers and names of the parcels; you know? So how could you overcome this, and how could we claim, those Palestinians, claim their properties, if there is a change in the records?

MR. SHAFI: Well, I would like to Professor Boyle's comment about this, but I would say that what we need is that Israel acknowledges Resolution 194 and express its decision to implement or participate in implementing this resolution, and then, I'm sure, through discussion, we can find the right way of implementing this resolution.

MR. BOYLE: I want to answer this question, then I'll recognize you, sir, because you had your hand up. Well, as we know, there are precedents here. The current precedent is the Jewish people right now are in negotiations with the German government, the Austrian government—apparently they're going to start with the French government—to try to do the best as possible to determine who owned what and why. Commissions have been set up under the auspices of the United States government; I should point out, to do this. The Swiss government has done it. It does not appear that most of the Jewish refugees from the Second World War and the Nazi Holocaust want to go back. That is their right. But they do want recognition of their property rights and compensation to be paid if property was taken. So I think there is adequate precedent here. I have not been retained by the provisional government of the state of Palestine to do this study. But there is more than adequate precedent for doing precisely what you're asking in the manner that Jewish claims have been handled after the Second World War. And there's been a good deal written about this and a lot of precedent going on.[7] So I think a study could be made and an agenda could be drawn up to do this.

Sir?

Q: Can we pursue that? And particularly, would you comment on what is a striking recent precedent for how one goes about funding compensation, and that is what was done by the United Nations vis-à-vis Iraq, where 30 percent of Iraq's foreign exchange earnings were sequestered and put into a compensation fund. Why could that not be considered as a way of funding the compensation claims by the Palestinians vis-à-vis Israel?

MR. BOYLE: I have already said, in my opinion—and I have advised the provisional government of the state of Palestine on this—that under the Uniting for Peace Resolution, the General Assembly can, if it wishes, adopt comprehensive economic sanctions on Israel. I did the memorandum for the provisional government of the state of Palestine on how to do this.[8] They have currently begun to invoke the Uniting for Peace Resolution. The last invocation was to have the General Assembly adopt a recommendation that no companies invest in occupied Palestinian lands. The session is currently in recess; it can be recalled, and they can move up the level of what sanctions might be applied.

In the Korean War, the United States government sponsored the Uniting for Peace Resolution, and we convinced the General Assembly to adopt comprehensive economic sanctions against North Korea. So yes, you are right this can be done, if they're not prepared to negotiate in good faith, yes.

The other mechanism, which I've also recommended to the provisional government of the state of Palestine, is to sue Israel at the International Court of Justice in The Hague. I personally gave that memorandum to President Arafat.[9] I haven't heard back from him yet. I take it that he's trying to see if he's going to get anywhere in these negotiations with the Israelis. But that is a second mechanism that is available to the provisional government of the state of Palestine.

To go back to the earlier question about who has the authority to negotiate, and again, Dr. Abdul Shafi has pointed out the blurring of authority here, but legally speaking, the Palestine National Council created a state in 1988. I was the legal advisor for that matter.[10] Today, the Palestinian state is recognized de jure by about 130 states. We have de facto recognition from almost all of Europe. And the only reason Europe has not recognized the Palestinian state is massive pressure applied by the United States. Even Europe has said, about a year ago, they are prepared to give de jure recognition to the Palestinian state. The only holdouts on de jure recognition for the Palestinian state are Israel and the United States. And even Israel is now coming around to the point of view that, yes, they will have to recognize the Palestinian state.

A year ago, the provisional government of the state of Palestine obtained de facto membership in the United Nations Organization. They have all the rights of a U.N. member state, except the right to vote. So they have international legal personality. They have presence and a voice at the United Nations. They have used mechanisms that are available, and there are further mechanisms that can be invoked if necessary, if Israel is not prepared to negotiate in good faith in accordance with two resolutions that they accepted as conditions for their membership in the United Nations Organization. And I have already done a memorandum for the provisional government of the state of Palestine, that their outright repudiation of 194 and 181 has violated the basic conditions for their membership in the United Nations Organization. And although they could not be formally suspended or expelled over a U.S. veto, nevertheless their participation in the General Assembly could be suspended. And their participation throughout the entirety of the United Nations Organization could be suspended, exactly what was done to the former apartheid government in South Africa and the current genocidal Yugoslavia. So these are very serious issues. There are severe consequences, some of which Dr. Abdul Shafi has pointed out. I am just here to address the legal issues.

Is there a further question before we adjourn? Thank you very much.

NOTES

1   Universal Declaration of Human Rights, Article 13(2) (1948).

2   *See* Francis A. Boyle, Palestine, Palestinians, and International Law 153-58 (2003) (hereinafter cited as *Palestine*).

3   Janine Zacharia, *Refugee Issue Threatens Israel's U.N. Standing,* Jerusalem Post, March 5, 2000.

4   *See* Francis A. Boyle, Breaking All the Rules: Palestine, Iraq, Iran, and the Case for Impeachment 31-32 (2008) (hereinafter cited as *Breaking*).

5   Salman Abu-Sitta, *The Feasibility of the Right of Return,* in The Palestinian Exodus 171-96 (Karmi & Eugene Cotran eds. : 1999).

6   *See, e.g.,* Ilan Pappe, The Ethnic Cleansing of Palestine (2006).

7   *See, e.g.,* Ben Ferencz, Less Than Slaves: Jewish Forced Labor and the Quest for Compensation (1979); Scott Leckie, Housing, Land and Property Restitution Rights of Refugees and Displaced Persons (2007).

8   Boyle, *Palestine, supra* at 35-39.

9   Francis A. Boyle, *Palestine: Sue Israel for Genocide Before the International Court of Justice !,* 20 J. Muslim Min. Aff. No. 1, at 161-66 (2000).

10   *See* Francis A. Boyle, *Palestine, supra* at 25-57; John Quigley, The Statehood of Palestine (2010).

Chapter 3

The Impending Collapse
of Israel in Palestine

Existing Recognition of the State of Palestine

On November 15, 1988 the Palestine National Council (P.N.C.) meeting in Algiers proclaimed the Palestinian Declaration of Independence that created the independent state of Palestine. Today the State of Palestine is bilaterally recognized de jure by about 130 states. Palestine has de facto diplomatic recognition from most states of Europe. It was only massive political pressure applied by the U.S. government that prevented European states from according de jure diplomatic recognition to Palestine.

Palestine is a member state of the League of Arab States and of the Organization of Islamic Conference (O.I.C.). When the International Court of Justice in The Hague—the World Court of the United Nations System—conducted its legal proceedings on Israel's apartheid wall on the West Bank, it invited the State of Palestine to participate in the proceedings. In other words, the International Court of Justice recognized the State of Palestine.

Palestine has Observer State Status with the United Nations Organization, and basically all the rights of a U.N. Member State except the right to vote. Effectively, Palestine has de facto U.N. Membership. The only thing keeping Palestine from de jure U.N. Membership is the implicit threat of a veto at the U.N. Security Council by the United States, which is clearly illegal because it would violate a solemn and binding pledge given by the United States not to veto States applying for U.N. Membership.[1] Someday, Palestine shall become a full-fledged U.N. Member State.

Palestinian Recognition of the 1947 U.N. Partition Resolution

From a world-order perspective, the 1988 Palestinian Declaration of Independence created a remarkable opportunity for peace with Israel because therein the P.N.C. explicitly accepted the U.N. General Assembly's Partition Resolution 181(II) of 1947 that called for the creation of a Jewish state and an Arab state in the Mandate for Palestine, together with an international trusteeship for the City of Jerusalem, in order to resolve their basic conflict:

Despite the historical injustice inflicted on the Palestinian Arab people resulting in their dispersion and depriving them of their right to self-determination following upon U.N. General Assembly Resolution 181 (1947), which partitioned Palestine into two states, one Arab, one Jewish, yet it is this Resolution that still provides those conditions of international legitimacy that ensure the right of the Palestinian Arab people to sovereignty and national independence. [2]

The significance of the P.N.C.'s acceptance of the Partition Resolution in the Palestinian Declaration of Independence itself could not be over-emphasized. Prior thereto, from the perspective of the Palestinian people, the Partition Resolution had been deemed to be a criminal act that was perpetrated upon them by the United Nations Organization in gross violation of their fundamental right to self-determination as recognized by the United Nations Charter and general principles of public international law. The acceptance of the Partition Resolution in their actual Declaration of Independence signaled the genuine desire by the Palestinian people to transcend the past century of bitter conflict with the Jewish people living illegally in their midst in order to reach an historic accommodation with them on the basis of a two-state solution.

The very fact that this acceptance of Partition Resolution 181 was set forth in their Declaration of Independence indicated the degree of sincerity with which the Palestinian people accepted the existence of Israel. The Declaration of Independence was intended to be the foundational document for the State of Palestine. It was intended to be determinative, definitive, and irreversible. As the P.N.C. sincerely believed and intended at the time, their Declaration of Independence was not something that they could amend or bargain away.

Recognizing "the Jewish State"

Nonetheless, the Palestinians then fruitlessly spent the next two decades trying to negotiate in good faith with Israel over establishing the two-state solution set forth in Resolution 181. They have gotten absolutely nowhere. Israel has never demonstrated even one iota of good faith when it came to negotiating a comprehensive Middle East peace settlement with the Palestinians on the basis of a two-state solution. Even the 1993 Oslo Agreement was nothing more than an Israeli-drafted interim Bantustan arrangement for five years that had been rejected in Washington, D.C. by the Palestinian Delegation to the Middle East Peace Negotiations for that precise reason. Both Israel and the United States now want to make the Oslo Bantustan permanent and incidental thereto, destroy the right of the Palestinian refugees to return to their homes as required by U.N. General Assembly Resolution

194 (III) of 1948 and general principles of public international law.

Shortly before he died on September 24, 2007, I called up the former Head of the Palestinian Delegation to the Middle East Peace Negotiations, Dr. Haidar Abdul Shaffi, at his home in Gaza in order to review the entire situation with him in a lengthy conversation. According to Dr. Haidar: "The Zionists have not changed their objectives since the Basel Conference of 1897!" In other words, the Zionists still want a "Greater" Israel over all of the Mandate for Palestine together with as much ethnic cleansing of Palestinians from their homes in Palestine as the Zionists believe they can get away with internationally.

Toward obtaining those genocidal ends, in a speech at the Begin-Sadat Center at Bar-Ilan University on June 14, 2009, Israel's Likudnik Prime Minister Benjamin Netanyahu reached into his bag of Zionist tricks and pulled out a brand-new demand that had never surfaced before in the history of the Middle East Peace Process going all the way back to its beginning with the negotiation of the original Camp David Accords conducted under the personal auspices of U.S. President Jimmy Carter in 1978: The Palestinians must now recognize Israel as "the Jewish State." Not surprisingly, the Zionist funded and controlled Obama administration publicly endorsed this latest roadblock to peace that was maliciously constructed by Israel, even as it seemed likely to derail that administration's own allegedly highly-desired effort to improve its own domestic and international standing and that of its rogue client state Israel by concluding a final peace agreement.

Netanyahu deliberately shifted the goal-posts on the Palestinians. It would be as if the United States of America demanded that Iran recognize it as the White Anglo-Saxon Protestant (WASP) State as a condition for negotiating and then concluding any comprehensive peace settlement with it. Or as if the white racist criminal apartheid regime in South Africa had demanded that Nelson Mandela and the African National Congress recognize it as the "Afrikaner State" as a condition for any peace settlement. Of course such demands are not only racist but premeditated non-starters to begin with.

Netanyahu's racist ultimatum was specifically intended to pave the way for the denationalization of the 1.5 million Palestinians who are already less than third-class citizens of Israel and set the stage for their mass expulsion to the Palestinian Bantustan envisioned by Netanyahu and Obama as the "final solution" to Zionism's "demographic problem" created by the very existence of the Palestinians.

This racist and genocidal demand would also illegally terminate the well-recognized Right of Return for five million Palestinian refugees living around the world as required by U.N. General Assembly Resolution 194(III) of 1948, by the Universal Declaration of Human Rights Article 13(2) (1948), and by general principles of public international law, international humanitarian law, and human rights law. This would doom all prospects for peace between Israelis and Palestinians forever, and lead directly to the creation of the "Greatest Israel" dominating the entire former Mandate for Palestine, both of which objectives have been the long-term design of Netanyahu and Likud and Rabin and Labor all along.

The State of the Jews—*Jewistan!*

But if Netanyahu is really serious about Israel being recognized internationally as "the Jewish State" then there is a simple manner by which this universal diplomatic status can instantly be achieved unilaterally by Israel, without the consent of the Palestinians, and on a worldwide basis. Under basic principles of international law, every state is free to change its own name if it so desires: e.g., from Congo to Zaire then back to Congo. Therefore Israel is free to change its name to Jewistan—the State of the Jews.

Thereafter every state in the world that has diplomatic relations and treaty relations with Israel will henceforth necessarily have to recognize it as Jewistan—the State of Jews—and deal with it as such by that name on a daily basis. The name of Jewistan would automatically replace the name of Israel throughout the United Nations System, at all other concerned international organizations, and on all bilateral and multilateral treaties to which Israel is currently a contracting party. In the aftermath of its serial and genocidal atrocities perpetrated against the Palestinians and the Lebanese, Israel has quite understandably been seeking to "re-brand" itself. Jewistan would be a perfect new moniker for Israel.

Israel as a Jewish Bantustan

In fact, "Israel" has never been anything but a Bantustan for Jews set up in the Middle East after the Second World War by the genocidal racist Western colonial/imperial powers who wished to severely limit the inflow of Jewish war refugees into their own states. Their intent was rather to force them to serve as Western imperialism's attack dog and genocidal enforcer against the Arab and Muslim world by locating them in Palestine, which has functioned as the strategically critical geographical crossroads of the Middle East ever since the Roman, Alexandrian, and Egyptian Empires. From the very moment of Western imperialism's genocidal conception of creating the client state of Israel by means of their Partition Resolution of 1947 and the *Nakba* of 1948, Israel has always functioned as a Bantustan for the Jews.

Israel would have never come into existence without the support of the Western colonial imperial powers throughout the twentieth century. In specific regard to the 1948 *Nakba*, "Israel" has never been a State but just a gang of terrorists masquerading as a state—a Potemkin

Village of a State—which is a good definition for a Bantustan. And the same principle still holds true today. Without the political, economic, diplomatic, and military support provided primarily by the United States, and to a lesser extent by Britain, France, and Germany, Israel would immediately collapse. As a matter of fact, as long ago as October 1973, Israel would have collapsed without the support of the United States during the so-called Yom Kippur War.[3] Nothing has changed during the interim. As recently as October 21, 2010, Israeli President Shimon Peres publicly stated at a press conference in Jerusalem that Israel could not even exist without the assistance of the United States.[4] And as the American Empire rapidly and inevitably continues its decline into decrepitude, so too the Jewish Bantustan will necessarily and pari passu plummet toward dissolution.

Foreseeing the Jewish Bantustan's Collapse

In light of these existential facts, after twenty-two years of getting nowhere but further screwed to Israel's apartheid wall on the West Bank and strangulated in Gaza, it is now time for the Palestinians to adopt a new strategy, which I most respectfully recommend here for them to consider: *Sign nothing and let the Jewish Bantustan in Palestine collapse!* Recently it was reported that the United States' own Central Intelligence Agency predicted the collapse of Israel within twenty years.[5] My most respectful advice to the Palestinians is to let the Jewish Bantustan in Palestine so collapse!

For the Palestinians to sign any type of comprehensive peace treaty with Israel would only shore up, consolidate, and guarantee the existence of Zionism and Zionists and their Jewish Bantustan in Palestine forever. Why would the Palestinians want to do that? Without approval by the Palestinians in writing on a comprehensive peace treaty and the legitimacy that this would confer upon Israel, opening the way to removal of its increasingly pariah status, Zionism and the Jewish Bantustan in Palestine will collapse. For that very reason the Palestinians must not sign any Middle East Peace Treaty with Israel, but instead must keep up the pressure on the Jewish Bantustan, emphasizing its illegitimacy and genocidal birth and criminal acts, in order to produce the collapse of Israel over the next two decades as predicted by the Central Intelligence Agency.

An Analogue: The Collapse of Yugoslavia

The correct historical analogue here is not apartheid South Africa,[6] but instead the genocidal Yugoslavia that collapsed as a State, lost its U.N. Membership, and now no longer exists as a State for that very reason. I was the lawyer for the Republic of Bosnia and Herzegovina during Yugoslavia's war of extermination against the Bosnians. On 8 April 1993 and 13 September 1993 I won two Orders of Provisional Measures of Protection from the International Court of Justice in The Hague that were overwhelmingly in favor of Bosnia. These Orders—the international equivalents of temporary restraining orders and injunctions combined—required Yugoslavia to cease and desist from committing all their acts of genocide against the Bosnians in violation of the 1948 Genocide Convention. The mighty Yugoslavia—deploying one of the most powerful armies in Europe that was originally designed by Tito to resist and repel an invasion from the Soviet Union after his break with Stalin—literally collapsed and disintegrated as a state and lost its U.N. Membership right before my very eyes. I was honored and privileged to have played a role in propelling this historical and principled process forward and ushering in the final extinction of the genocidal Yugoslavia as a state by debunking its legal, moral, and political right to survive and exist in front of the entire world for all humanity to see. [7] The exact same legal, political, moral, and historical forces are now in operation that will result in the extinction of the genocidal Bantustan for Jews in Palestine, otherwise known as Israel.

It is a matter of historical record that the self-same racist Western colonial imperial powers that artificially concocted the genocidal Jewish Bantustan in Palestine had similarly previously concocted the artificial State of Yugoslavia at their 1919 Paris "Peace"/ Diktat Conference after the First World War in order to serve as their racist attack dog and genocidal enforcer for the Balkans. *Plus ça change, plus ça reste la même chose.* Originally they had baptized what was to become the genocidal Yugoslavia with the moniker "Kingdom of the Serbs, Croats and Slovenes" to the obvious exclusion of the Bosnian Muslims. The Western imperialist powers thus paved the way for the latter's extermination by the genocidal Yugoslavia in the 1990s that I have so desperately fought to stop (see Appendix 2).

Waging Lawfare

Two decades ago human rights lawyers all over the world mobilized in order to hunt down and prosecute Yugoslav war criminals wherever they might be—just like a generation ago Jewish lawyers hunted down and prosecuted Nazi war criminals after World War II. Similarly, today human rights lawyers all over the world are now mobilizing in order to hunt down and prosecute Israeli war criminals wherever they might travel abroad.

In these modern human rights campaigns we lawyers have made extensive use of the anti-Nazi Nuremberg Charter (1945), Nuremberg Judgment (1946), and Nuremberg Principles (1950) to go after Yugoslav and Israeli war criminals. [8] It has finally reached such a sustained level that Israeli political officials and military personnel must now seek formal Legal Advice from their government lawyers about where they can safely travel without getting prosecuted. Several such official Israeli war criminals have had to cancel foreign trips or leave a country abruptly for fear of prosecution.

These human rights lawsuits against Israeli war criminals have already exerted a profoundly negative political and strategic impact upon Israel. On November 3, 2010 it was publicly announced that Britain and Israel had mutually agreed to suspend their "High-Level U.K.-Israel Strategic Dialogue" because Israel had to stop sending officials to Britain for fear of their criminal prosecution.[9] Needless to say, it was the white racist imperial colonial power Britain that had started the entire problem of Zionism in Palestine in the first place by means of its 1917 Balfour Declaration that illegally promised the Jews a "national home" in Palestine. Britain had no right to steal or assign even one square millimeter of Palestine from the Palestinians and give it to the Jews!

Like the Nazi war criminals before them, these Israeli and Yugoslav war criminals are *hostes humani generis*—the enemies of all humankind! And there is no Statute of Limitations for the commission of international crimes by Israelis, Yugoslavs, Nazis, or anyone else for that matter. Human rights lawyers all over the world will hunt down and prosecute Israeli and Yugoslav war criminals for the rest of their natural lives—just as today Jewish lawyers still hunt down and prosecute geriatric Nazi war criminals 65 years after the termination of the Second World War. Sauce for the goose is sauce for the gander!

Boycott/Divestment Power

Furthermore, the International Campaign for Boycott, Divestment, and Sanctions (B.D.S.) against Israel is quickly whittling away Zionism's domestic support in the same white racist genocidal Western colonial imperial powers such as Britain which were the Jewish Bantustan's original progenitors and remain its only sources of sustenance in the world today. The danger this poses to Israel has been acknowledged by Netanyahu himself. As recently as October 24, 2010 Jerry Silverman, President and C.E.O. of the Jewish Federation of North America (J.F.N.A.) which includes the United States and Canada—quite tellingly conceded: "In fact... Israeli leaders indentify this [B.D.S.] as the second most dangerous threat to Israel, after Iran's pursuit of nuclear weapons."[10]

On November 30, 2000, I gave a speech at Illinois State University that founded and launched the now worldwide Israeli Divestment/Disinvestment Campaign.[11] Only now have the J.F.N.A. and the Jewish Council for Public Affairs decided to launch a $6 million dollar campaign over the next three years to counteract the rapidly-expanding B.D.S. Movement in North America. Too little and too late!

The B.D.S. genie is long out of the bottle.

The Zionists and their Jewish Bantustan in Palestine can be defeated. I have repeatedly done so myself by means of using international law and human rights because thereunder Zionists and their Jewish Bantustan in Palestine have no defense, no excuse, and no justification. The Zionists and their Jewish Bantustan in Palestine do not have a leg to stand upon, and they know it. Israel's recent serial and barbarous atrocities perpetrated against the Palestinians and the Lebanese have revealed the true face of Zionism and its Jewish Bantustan for the entire world to see: it is the Face of Genocide.

Another "Ism" to Bite the Dust

So it has become obvious to the entire world and even and especially to America's own C.I.A. that soon Zionism and its Jewish Bantustan in Palestine will enter into Trotsky's "dustbin" of history along with every other aggressive and genocidal nationalistic "ism" that has plagued humankind during the twentieth century: Nazism, Fascism, Francoism, Phalangism, Stalinism, Maoism, etc. The only thing that could possibly save Zionism and its Jewish Bantustan in Palestine is for the Palestinians to conclude any type of so-called comprehensive Middle East Peace treaty with Israel. It is this very understanding—that Israel must make peace with the Palestinians in order to survive—that has led the Obama administration to risk public rupture with the Jewish Bantustan's government in an effort to bring it about. Conversely then, it is for precisely this reason that the Palestinians must sign nothing with Israel and let the Jewish Bantustan collapse of its own racist and genocidal weight over the next two decades if not much sooner. **In the meantime, the Palestinians must stall and delay the so-called peace negotiations until then!** Time is on their side.

Zionism Fatigue

All the demographic forces are in favor of the Palestinians and against the Zionists in Palestine.[12] The American military-industrial complex and its concomitant power elite are weary of their blank-check support for Israel because this myopic policy seriously undermines and directly conflicts with their post-9/11 overall imperial strategy to steal all the oil and gas lying beneath Arab and Muslim states by hook or by crook. Israel is ridden with and paralyzed by so many internal contradictions and conflicts that they are too numerous to list here. As a result, the Jewish Bantustan is ineluctably moving towards a Civil War among Zionists of multiple and diametrically opposed persuasions. Israel's implosion is now concatenating.

Endgame: Sign Nothing, Win It All!

These legal, political, economic, military, diplomatic, sociological, psychological, and demographic forces are all working in favor of the Palestinians and against the Jewish Bantustan and the Zionists in Palestine. It will take a few more years for these historical forces to predominate and then to prevail. But the proverbial handwriting is on the wall for the Zionist Enterprise in Palestine for the entire world to see, including and especially the C.I.A. Even large numbers of Zionists living in Israel have already prepared their parachutes, their exit plans, and their landing zones elsewhere in the world. There is no reason for the Palestinians to give the Zionists and their Jewish Bantustan a new lease on life in Palestine by signing any sort of peace treaty with Israel.

Millions of Palestinians have waited in refugee camps since 1948, that is, for 62 years, in order to return to their homes. They can wait a little longer until the Jewish Bantustan in Palestine collapses sometime during the next two decades. But if the Palestinians sign a comprehensive peace treaty with Israel now they will *never* be able to return to their homes as guaranteed by Resolution 194 of 1948. Netanyahu along with the Zionist funded and controlled Obama administration envision a Comprehensive "Peace" Plan for the Palestinians that will constitute a Second *Nakba*—another Catastrophe for them. The Peace of the Grave.

History, demography and legitimacy are all on the side of Palestine and the Palestinians working against "Israel" and its Gang of Zionist terrorists. But the Palestinians must allow history, demography and legitimacy a little bit more time in order to produce the collapse of Zionism and its Jewish Bantustan in Palestine. Twenty years is but the blink of an eye in the millennia-long history of the Palestinian people, who are the original indigenous inhabitants of Palestine.

"God" had no right to steal Palestine from the Palestinians and give Palestine to the Jews to begin with. A fortiori the United Nations had no right to steal Palestine from the Palestinians and give Palestine to the Zionists in 1947. A priori its predecessor the League of Nations had no right to steal Palestine from the Palestinians and give it to Britain with a so-called "Mandate" incorporating the illegal Balfour Declaration in order to facilitate the Zionist invasion, colonization, occupation, and conquest of Palestine, together with the genocidal ethnic cleansing of the Palestinians from their homes and land.

In the meantime, the Palestinians must ratchet up the pressure on Israel, Zionism, and the Zionists in Palestine and around the world. The Palestinians have a perfect right under international law to resist an illegal, colonial, genocidal, criminal, military occupation regimé of their lands and of their homes and of their people by the Jewish Bantustan in Palestine that goes all the way back to 1948 in all manners that are consistent with the requirements of international humanitarian law. Simultaneously, the Palestinians must continue to build their state from the ground up as they have been doing quite successfully since the first Intifada began in 1987 with its grassroots organization of the Unified Leadership of the Intifada.

Internationally, the Palestinians must continue their diplomatic, political and legal offensive against Israel, including and especially our campaign of Lawfare. International law is the most powerful weapon the Palestinians have in their arsenal! Palestine has gained enormous legal, moral, and political ground against Israel since November 15, 1988 when the P.N.C. proclaimed the independent State of Palestine. Palestine will continue to gain more support internationally over the next two decades, especially by means of the now accelerating B.D.S. campaign that will progressively delegitimize, undermine, undercut, and debunk the Jewish Bantustan, Zionism and Zionists all over the world.[13] At the same time, Israel will continue its precipitous descent into pariah-state status along the lines of the genocidal Yugoslavia that collapsed as a State, lost its U.N. Membership, and no longer exists as a State for that very reason. Israel will suffer the same fate as the now defunct genocidal Yugoslavia provided the Palestinians do not sign any type of international peace agreement with the Jewish Bantustan in Palestine.

When Israel collapses, most Zionists will have already left or will soon leave for other places around the world, many of which may be their actual states of origin. The Palestinians will then be able to claim *all* of the historic Mandate for Palestine as their State, including the entire City of Jerusalem as their capital. *Palestine will then be able to invite all of its refugees scattered around the world to return to their homes pursuant to Resolution 194!* That in a nutshell is the ultimate solution for implementing and achieving the Palestinian right of return under international law.

Some Jews will remain in Palestine either voluntarily or involuntarily. Palestine and the Palestinians will treat the remaining Jews fairly. Palestine and the Palestinians will not do to the Jews what Israel, Zionism, and the Zionists have done to the Palestinians.

The Palestinians must sign nothing and let the Jewish Bantustan in Palestine collapse!
Free Palestine—all of it!

Endnotes

1   *See* Louis B. Sohn, Cases on United Nations' Law 82-83 (2d ed. rev. 1967).
2   *See* Francis A. Boyle, Palestine, Palestinians and International Law 44 (2003).
3   Ethan Bronner, *Transcripts on '73 War, Now Public, Grip Israel,* New York Times, Oct. 11, 2010.
4   *Peres: Israel Could Not Exist Without the U.S.,* Jpost.com Staff, Oct. 22, 2010.

5   Michael Krebs, *CIA Report Predicts Israeli Collapse in 20 Years, Exodus to U.S.*, Digital Journal, March 15, 2009.

6   *But see* Ali Abunimah, One Country (2006).

7   *See Trying to Stop Aggressive War and Genocide Against the People and the Republic of Bosnia and Herzegovina* in Appendix 2 *infra. See also* Francis A. Boyle, The Bosnian People Charge Genocide! (1996).

8   [Francis A. Boyle], *Memorandum on the Yaron Case*, 5 Palestine Y.B. Int'l L. 254, 257 (1989).

9   *See* Tobias Buck & James Blitz, *Spat Mars Hague's Israel Visit*, Financial Times, Nov. 3, 2010; *Israel Halts Strategic Talks with U.K. over Lawsuits*, Reuters, Nov. 3, 2010.

10   Jacob Berkman, *Federations, JCPA Teaming to Fight Delegitimization of Israel*, JTA.org, Oct. 24, 2010.

11   *See Palestine, Palestinians and International Law* in Appendix 1 *infra*.

12   Arnon Soffer, *Jewish Population in Israel Is Declining*, Haaretz.com, Oct. 4, 2010.

13   *See generally* Joel Kovel, Overcoming Zionism (2007).

APPENDIX 1

McMaster University

The Centre for Peace Studies McMaster University

presents

The 18th Annual Bertrand Russell Peace Lectures

The Legacy of Bertrand Russell: Principle Confronting Power

Francis Boyle

Francis A. Boyle is a leading American professor, practitioner and advocate of international law. He was responsible for drafting the Biological Weapons Anti-Terrorism Act of 1989. He served as legal advisor to the Palestinian Delegation to the Middle East Peace Negotiations from 1991 to 1993, served on the Board of Directors of Amnesty International from 1988 to 1992, and represented Bosnia-Herzegovina at the World Court.

Professor Boyle teaches international law at the University of Illinois, Champaign and is the author of numerous works, including The Future of International Law and American Foreign Policy (1989), Palestine, Palestinians and International Law (2003), and Destroying World Order: U.S. Imperialism in the Middle East Before and After September 11th (2004).

Palestine, Palestinians and International Law
Tuesday, January 9, 2007

The U.S. National Campaign to Impeach President George W. Bush Jr.
Wednesday, January 10, 2007

7:30 pm Room 1A1, Ewart Angus Centre
McMaster University

Funding for this lecture series is provided in part by the Keith Leppmann Memorial Fund.

Palestine, Palestinians and International Law

Introduction

Thank you Atif for that very fine introduction. First, on a personal note I want to say how happy I am to be here lecturing again in Canada. My mother's maiden name is Monarque and that branch of our family comes from Montreal. Her grandfather, George André Monarque, emigrated from Montreal to Chicago in 1864. So it is always nice to have a Monarque come back to Canada.

Of course I'm greatly honored to be chosen as a Bertrand Russell Peace Lecturer because Russell was one of my boyhood heroes, as was anyone who opposed the genocidal war against Vietnam—especially the important work that Russell did in organizing that path-breaking Tribunal that was so important in turning international public opinion against that terrible, criminal war, particularly in the United States. In addition, of course was the importance of the Russell/Einstein Manifesto on Nuclear Weapons. Given all the work I've done against nuclear weapons now for thirty years, the Russell/Einstein manifesto was a seminal event in the anti-nuclear movement. Today, I was privileged to have been shown in the Russell archive the original acceptance of the Manifesto, signed by Einstein himself. It was a real treat.

Bertrand Russell and the Middle East

In my preparation for this lecture, the archivists also informed me of some of Russell's positions on the Middle East, which I asked for and with which they kindly provided me. It turned out his very last message was on the Middle East, which I thought would be most appropriate tonight, and I've asked it to be distributed as a handout. [*See* Handout 1 reprinted at the end of this section.] Let me point out, in particular, paragraph three, I won't quote all of it, but it still has bearing today: "For over 20 years," here he's writing in 1970, "Israel has expanded by force of arms. After every stage in this expansion Israel has appealed to 'reason' and has suggested 'negotiations.' This is the traditional way of the imperial power because it wishes to consolidate

71

with the least difficulty what it has already taken by violence. Every new conquest becomes the new basis of proposed negotiation from strength, which ignores the injustice of the previous aggression." Well of course as I will comment on later, that was certainly my experience serving as legal advisor to the Palestinian delegation to the Middle East peace negotiations from their beginning in 1991, to their end in 1993, and still, in trying to help the Palestinians today.

But I was struck by the date of this last statement of his life on 31 January 1970, just about the time when I, as a young man, commenced my studies of the Middle East at the University of Chicago with Professor Leonard Binder—the first week of January 1970, Winter Quarter, thirty-seven years ago, now. Professor Binder was very fair, and balanced and reasonable in his presentation of the positions on all sides. At the end of this quarter of study—and a very fine course and instructor—I had reached the conclusion that the only way there could be peace in the Middle East would be if the Palestinians had their own state as originally promised to them in the Partition Resolution 181 by the United Nations General Assembly. And that perhaps someday I might have a role to play in bringing about that Palestinian state and also in promoting peace in the Middle East.

The 1988 Palestinian Declaration of Independence

Jumping forward seventeen years to 1987, the United Nations decided to have a Commemoration of the 20th Anniversary of the Six Day War and the Palestine Liberation Organization asked me to speak at U.N. Headquarters on their behalf. In that speech, I said that the time had now come for the Palestinians to create their own state, to move forward with that state, to seek United Nations' recognition, and then from the position of that statehood to enter into negotiations with Israel on the basis of a two-state solution. The P.L.O. liked what I had to say, asked me to write it up in a position paper, and when King Hussein of Jordan severed all ties with the West Bank and the Gaza Strip on July 31, 1988 (as a result of the first Intifada), I became legal advisor to the Palestine Liberation Organization on the Palestinian Declaration of Independence and their Peace Initiative of 15 November 1988.

Today, the Palestinian state is recognized de jure by about 130 states. It is recognized de facto by all of the member states of the European community, which has promised it de jure recognition. The only thing that has prevented the European states from recognizing the Palestinian state is the massive pressure applied by the United States.

Today, the state of Palestine has de facto United Nations membership, it has all the rights of a U.N. member state except the right to vote. It has all the votes to be admitted as a state to the United Nations. The only thing keeping it out is the threat of a veto by the United States.

Finally, even President Bush in his so-called Road Map has called for a Palestinian state and even former Prime Minister Ariel Sharon in a debate in the Knesset on this point, said to his opponents, "look, the Palestinians already have their state." And they do. The debate now is what type of state this is going to be. Is it going to be an independent, viable state or will it be a bantustan along the lines of what the former criminal apartheid regime in South Africa attempted to impose upon the Black people in South Africa? Here in North America we call our bantustans Indian reservations, but it's pretty much the same idea. That is what the issue is now. Will it be a real Palestinian state or will it be a bantustan?

The 1988 Palestinian Peace Initiative

Now let me go back and explore the start of the Middle East Peace Process. This was not the idea of the United States, it was the idea of the Palestinians—this Peace Initiative, as part of their Declaration of Independence.

1) First and foremost the Declaration of Independence accepted in name U.N. General Assembly Partition Resolution 181 of 1947, calling for two states—a Jewish state and an Arab state with a separate international status for the city of Jerusalem. The fact that this acceptance of the Partition Resolution was in the very Declaration of Independence itself demonstrated the degree of sincerity that the Palestinian people had. This Declaration of Independence was proclaimed by the Palestine National Council itself, meeting in Algiers and representing not only the Palestinians living in occupied Palestine but all Palestinians living around the world. And on the evening of Independence Day it was also proclaimed in front of Al Aqsa Mosque on Haram Al-Sharif in Jerusalem, the capital of the new Palestinian state, hence showing both the political and the religious significance of the Al-Aqsa Mosque. The second Intifada was called the Al-Aqsa Intifada. I will return to that later.

2) In the Declaration of Independence, the Palestine National Council declared its commitment to the Purposes and Principles of the United Nations Charter, the Universal Declaration of Human Rights, and the policies and principles of nonalignment.

3) In the Declaration of Independence, the Palestine National Council—remember not just the P.L.O., but the representatives of all the Palestinian people living around the world—declared that without prejudice to its natural right to defend the state of Palestine, it rejected "the threat or use of force, violence and intimidation against its territorial integrity, and political independence or those of any other state"—meaning Israel.

4) In the Political Communiqué attached to the Declaration of Independence, the Palestine National Council indicated its willingness to have a United Nations trusteeship imposed on the state of Palestine as a temporary measure, under Chapter XII of the U.N. Charter. Again, this was intended to be yet another confidence building step with respect to Israel.

5) In the Political Communiqué, the Palestine National Council accepted U.N. Security Council Resolutions 242 [concerning withdrawal of Israeli armed forces from territories occupied in the 1967 conflict, termination of all claims or states of belligerency, respect for the right of every state in the area to live in peace within secure and recognised boundaries, and a just settlement of the refugee problem] and 338 [calling for the implementation of Resolution 242 in all its parts as well as for the commencement of comprehensive Middle East Peace negotiations] —going back to the war of 1967 on which of course Russell was commenting in that 1970 statement; and also the war of 1973, which gave rise to Resolution 338. Those borders are the so-called green line. There is a very good editorial today in the *New York Times* by an Israeli geographer saying: "it's a good thing we're going back to the green line." You can read it today online if you want to, this is an Israeli speaker, an Israeli Professor. The green line borders enclosed 24 percent more than the land allocated to the Jewish state by the Partition Resolution 181. So the Palestinians indicated they were prepared to accept 24 percent less land than was allocated to them by the United Nations. It is fair to say today that the only internationally recognized boundaries between Israel and Palestine are those of the Partition Resolution 181 of 1947, not the green line of 1967, which is nothing more than an armistice ceasefire line.

6) The Political Communiqué also indicated that it would be prepared to have the Palestinian state have some type of confederal link with Jordan in a confederal state. This is something that at the time was being called for by the Peace Plan of 1982 advocated by President Reagan. Again the Palestinians undertook this step as a confidence building gesture towards Israel.

7) In the Political Communiqué, the P.N.C. "once again states its rejection of terrorism in all its forms, including state terrorism." Saying basically: "yes, we reject terrorism ourselves, but we expect Israel to do the same." Well eventually, as you know, President Arafat then made a series of statements in Geneva further outlining that commitment to the rejection of terrorism. That led then on December 14, 1988 to President Ronald Reagan himself—a real Conservative—authorizing the start of a diplomatic dialogue with the Palestine Liberation Organization as the representative of the Palestinian people. That diplomatic dialogue, which is really de facto diplomatic recognition, continues today as we speak.

8) Finally, we have Secretary of State Jim Baker, publicly stating at that time, that the Israeli government will probably have to begin negotiating a peace settlement directly with the P.L.O., because all the Palestinian people living in Palestine and abroad recognize the P.L.O. as their sole and legitimate representative. That statement by Baker, and later, an April 3, 1989 statement by President George Bush Sr. that Israel should end its occupation of Arab lands and that the Palestinians must be given their political rights by means of an international peace conference, would lead to the convocation of the international peace negotiations for the Middle East, convened by the Bush Sr. administration starting in Madrid and then continuing on in Washington.

The Middle East Peace Negotiations

So notice who paved the groundwork here for the Middle East peace negotiations: it was not the Americans, it was not the Israelis, it was the Palestinians. It was their Declaration of Independence and their Political Communiqué that set the parameters for comprehensive Middle East peace negotiations between Israel, the Palestinians, Jordan, Lebanon, and Syria that opened in the Fall of 1991.

I was the legal advisor to the Palestinian delegation to the Middle East peace negotiations during that period of time—to the entire team, and especially the head of the team, His Excellency Dr. Haider Abdul Shaffi, who is still my client and my friend.* Since the Syrian team was also staying at the Grand Hotel in Washington with the Palestinians, the Syrians asked me to advise them as well. And I did advise them during the first round in the negotiations held in Washington. I've had no further contact with Syria since that time.

---

*He died on September 24, 2007. R.I.P.

So I was in a very unusual situation. Everyone knew that the Jordanians were fully prepared to negotiate a comprehensive peace settlement with Israel, but of course they couldn't go first. Everyone also knew that the Lebanese team unfortunately had to do whatever the Syrians told them to do. The Lebanese were under occupation by Syria at the time, courtesy of the United States government going back to Kissinger and then later President George Bush Sr., who awarded Lebanon as some type of a consolation prize to Syrian President Hafez al-Assad for helping him in his original aggression against Iraq. So unfortunately, Jordan and Lebanon were not much of a factor in those negotiations. But I was advising both the Syrians and the Palestinians, and they were really the key actors with respect to their separate negotiations with Israel.

Shamir's Stall-Job

We went there, the Palestinian team and, I would say, the Syrian team, in good faith to negotiate in accordance with the Letters of Agreement and Assurances that had been sent out to all the parties by Secretary of State Jim Baker, and I won't go through all those here. But when we got there in Washington, there were **no** reasonable, good faith negotiations at all by Israel. They would not even walk into the negotiating room with the Palestinians. They refused. Indeed, later on Prime Minister Shamir of the Likud party publicly stated that his strategy was to stall and delay these negotiations for the next ten years at least. Having been part of the process I can assure you that's exactly what the Israelis did. Indeed, with respect to the Palestinians and the Syrians, they're still doing it today.

Now it didn't surprise me that Israel stalled and delayed. But what did surprise me—I guess I was somewhat naïve—was that Baker did nothing. No pressure was applied on Israel to do anything. In the negotiations that Baker relegated to Dennis Ross—pretty much a spokesperson for the Israel lobby—nothing happened. Throughout the course of these negotiations Ross was basically a spear-carrier for the Israeli government. You can read his pathetic little piece in today's *New York Times* attacking President Carter. Afterwards, he went back to the Israeli lobby think-tank, where he originally came from. At least the others, such as Aaron Miller, came out and finally admitted this—he was working with Ross: "yes basically we were just spear-carriers for Israel. We made a mistake." So the State Department people in charge of this process went along with the Israeli agenda.[1]

State Department Prevarication

Not only did the State Department go along with it, but they lied to the Palestinians as to the meaning of the English legal documents that they had drafted, that they were trying to get the Palestinians to accept. I have that story in my book. You can read it there with the footnotes. All the materials I'm referring to are in my *Palestinian* book. The Palestinians would bring me these documents together with their mem-coms—the memorandums of conversation—with Djerejian or Ross or Miller etc. and say: "Well, they told us the documents meant this." And I said: "Well, that just isn't true. It's plain English, this is what it means." So I would straighten out the real meaning of the document, and then they would go back. They lied to the Palestinians about what these documents meant. They were drafted of course in English, Oslo was in English too, all negotiations, everything was in English.

So nothing happened despite the fact that before I showed up in the Grand Hotel, I had been instructed by the Palestinian Delegation to prepare position papers on every issue that was expected to come up in the peace negotiations and to develop a reasonable compromise that would protect their interests while also meeting the reasonable demands and interests of Israel. All that paperwork was there, it was done, it was ready to go. Nothing happened. Ross and Miller went right ahead and carried the water for the Israeli negotiators.

The Syrian Track

Now there then was a breakthrough, however, in Israel. The Likud lost the elections in the spring of 1992. Labor came to power. They elected a former general, Yitzhak Rabin, Prime Minister. One of Prime Minister Rabin's first steps on the peace process was to fire the entire Likud team of negotiators for Syria, and bring in Professor Rabinovich, who was and still is Israel's leading expert on Syria. Now at this point I was no longer advising the Syrians, but I knew exactly what their position was. Very rapid progress was made between Professor Rabinovich and the Syrian negotiators on a comprehensive peace treaty between Israel and Syria that was modeled on the peace treaty between Israel and Egypt. I know that because the Syrians asked me to draft their opening position to that effect.

Murdering Rabin

Prime Minister Rabin then indicated that the Syrian treaty would be signed after the 1996 election. Then they assassinated Prime Minister Rabin. His own people. Why? Because the military-industrial-security-complex in Israel did not want peace with Syria. It's that simple. And they still don't. It's very much like the military-industrial-security-complex that runs the United States. They don't want peace either. They have a vested interest in conflict and war. So Rabin was murdered.

Personally, I think if Rabin had lived and had won the election (which he was predicted to do), today there would have been a comprehensive peace settlement between Israel and Syria and of course President Hafez al-Assad would have had to have delivered Lebanon as part of the package. And the Lebanese would have signed whatever peace treaty they were told to sign by Israel, Syria, and the United States.

Now think about that. What if in 1996 we had had comprehensive peace treaties between Israel and Egypt going back to the Camp David Accords, Israel and Syria, Israel and Jordan, and Israel and Lebanon? Then all that would be left would have been further negotiations between Israel and the Palestinians. A remarkable situation, unfortunately not the case today, where last summer [2006] we saw the massive slaughter of Lebanese and Palestinians by Israel and Israel is still threatening war against Syria.

The Palestinian Track

Now Prime Minister Rabin did not, however, change the Likudnik negotiating team for the Palestinian track. Unfortunately, this was not a good sign. It did appear of course that he was willing to engage in a comprehensive peace treaty with Syria—Syria was a military power, and the Syrians were willing to cut a deal like Egypt had done. But Rabin hadn't really figured out what he was going to do with the Palestinians, and unfortunately kept the Likudnik team.

In the summer of 1992, finally, the Likudnik team produced a document that they tendered to the peace delegation in Washington. Dr. Haider Abdul Shaffi asked me to come out and analyze this document for the team. I had been in charge of analyzing all the previous Israeli peace offers going back to the Camp David Accords and the Linowitz Negotiations under President Carter that many people have forgotten. I arrived, I got the document, and they said to me: "Tell us what is the closest historical analog to what they are offering us in this document."

Israel's Bantustan Offer

I went back to my hotel room, and I spent the whole day studying it. I came back the next day and I said to them: "A bantustan. They are offering you a bantustan." Very similar to the legal chicanery that the Afrikaner criminal apartheid regime had imposed upon the Blacks in South Africa. I went through it point by point why this was a Bantustan, or again similar to what we North Americans call Indian Reservations—fake states. I also pointed out to the Palestinian team that this document carried out Prime Minister Begin's disingenuous misinterpretation of the Camp David Accords, rejected by President Jimmy Carter, that all they called for was autonomy for the Palestinian people and not for the land as well. Under this document, Palestinians had no real control over their land.

Finally, and even worse yet, and this was devised by Israeli lawyers whom I knew—whom I had debated, had confronted, etc. on all these issues so they knew what they were doing—Israel's proposed Palestinian interim self-government that we still see in existence today would be legally set up to function as the civilian arm of the Israeli military occupation forces. An occupying army can, if it wants to, set up a puppet government to carry out the occupation—and that's how this interim government was set up.

The Palestinian Counteroffer

I went home. I wasn't asked whether they should accept it or reject it. But they met and they rejected it, with the full support of President Arafat and the Central Committee of the P.L.O. Dr. Abdul Shaffi then invited me to come back. He was in a dilemma. They had rejected the Israeli bantustan proposal. But President Arafat basically said: "Fine, you have to come up with an alternative. What's the alternative to the Israeli bantustan proposal?" So Dr. Abdul Shaffi called me into his suite and said: "Professor Boyle we have decided to ask you to draft this interim peace agreement for us. Do whatever you want, but do not sell out our right to our state!" Those were his direct words.

So I proceeded to draft a counteroffer that would not be a bantustan for the Palestinians; that would provide for a genuine interim self-government arrangement for five years; that would then lead to the consolidation of an independent Palestinian state. Again you can read this counteroffer in my book. It was approved by President Arafat. It was approved by the Central Committee of the P.L.O. And the team then in Washington was negotiating on the basis of this anti-bantustan proposal.

Israel's Oslo Bantustan

Well, what happened? Without telling anyone on the negotiating team in Washington, the Israelis took their bantustan proposal up to Norway. Working with the Norwegian government as their partners in crime and with the cooperation of the United States government, they opened up a secret channel of negotiations in Norway.[2] President Arafat sent two of his emissaries, Abu Mazen, who is now the President of the Palestinian State, President Abbas, and Abu Ala who later became the Prime Minister of the Palestinian Authority. The Israelis then retendered their bantustan proposal in Norway. It was the exact same document we had rejected in Washington, D.C. with the approval of President Arafat and the P.L.O. Central Committee.

It was that Israeli bantustan proposal that became the Oslo agreement. Exactly the way the Israeli lawyers had written it, except Abu Mazen and Abu Ala were careful to add that all matters would be subject to negotiation in the final status negotiations including refugees, water, Jerusalem, etc. They would all be open and this could not prejudice the final status negotiations. It was that bantustan draft by Israel that President Arafat signed on the White House steps on 13 September 1993.

Why Did President Arafat Sign Israel's Oslo Bantustan?

Now you might ask yourself: Why did President Arafat accept a bantustan? Well, I didn't ask him. I know Dr. Abul Shaffi argued with him quite vigorously against it, but again President Arafat was the democratically elected leader of the Palestinian people, not us.

I believe President Arafat felt in good faith that he had to take this bantustan offered to him by Israel and the United States, and prove the good faith of the Palestinian people in this trial period of five years, prove that they wanted to live with Israel in peace, respect, and equality. But at the end of the five years, they would then get their state.

So if you read the scholarly analyses, many mistakenly say that President Arafat didn't know what he was signing. He knew exactly what he was signing. I told him and you can see my Memorandum to him in this book, *Palestine, Palestinians and International Law*.[3]

In fairness again to President Arafat, the Oslo agreement

indeed made it quite clear that all issues, including Jerusalem, would be open to negotiations in the final status negotiations. Also in fairness to President Arafat, the Palestine National Council had already adopted a resolution authorizing the P.L.O. to take control of any portion of occupied Palestine that was offered to them. So they accepted the Israeli bantustan and moved into Palestine.

President Arafat Rejects a Palestinian Civil War

Despite the fact that this was a bantustan, and the Palestinian Authority pretty much operated like a bantustan, to his great and undying credit, President Arafat refused to set off a Palestinian civil war. That was obviously what the Americans and the Israelis expected him to do—to serve as a Buthelezi figure, who would set off a Palestinian civil war in the name of the Oslo bantustan. He wouldn't do it. So they got rid of President Arafat. Personally, I believe he was poisoned. By the way, the only person who really had the credibility to produce a comprehensive peace settlement between Israel and Palestine was President Arafat.

The Camp David II Negotiations in 2000

I'm not going to waste my time going through all the agreements after Oslo, because I'm a professor of international law and not of bantustan law. But we bring the story then up to the Camp David II negotiations in the summer of 2000 where President Clinton, acting at the behest of Israeli Prime Minister Barak, decided to have peace negotiations. It was clear the agenda was to impose this Oslo bantustan on the Palestinians as the permanent solution. The permanent bantustan. Of course, President Arafat rejected a bantustan as the final solution. He held out for a genuine, independent Palestinian state that was not a bantustan.

The Al-Aqsa Intifada

What happened? At that point, the Israeli government under Barak and General Sharon concluded that that bantustan was their bottom line, and they were going to terminate peace negotiations, for good. So on 28 September 2000 General Ariel Sharon, the Butcher of Beirut, the architect of the Israeli invasion of Lebanon, the man who had exterminated 20,000 Arabs in Lebanon, including 2000 completely innocent women, children, and old men at Sabra and Shatilla, some of whom were my clients,[4] appeared at Al-Haram Al-Sharif, where you have the Dome of the Rock and the Al-Aqsa Mosque. The importance of the Al-Aqsa, again, to the Palestinians, is that it is the third holiest site in Islam. Sharon desecrated the Haram Al-Sharif by bringing 100 armed Israeli troops in a provocation, and then the next day the Israelis shot dead several Palestinians. Shot them dead like dogs in the street.

Thus commenced the Al-Aqsa Intifada, the Intifada to defend the Al-Aqsa Mosque. This was a deliberate provocation by Barak and Sharon, heads of the two parties, Labor and Likud, to head off any peace and negotiating process. All the death and destruction that we have seen there since between Israel, on the one hand, and Palestine on the other, go back to this desecration of Haram Al-Sharif by Ariel Sharon with the full approval of Barak.

Indeed, you don't have to accept my word for it. On 7 October 2000 the United Nations Security Council adopted Resolution 1322. The United States government could have vetoed this resolution but did not. It abstained. And paragraph one of this resolution, adopted 14 to 0 with 1 abstention, says the Security Council "deplores the provocation carried out at Al-Haram Al-Sharif in Jerusalem on 28 September 2000 and the subsequent violence there."

The Israeli Divestment/Disinvestment Campaign

It was clear to me at this point that Israel, Labor and Likud, the two leading parties, had decided to terminate peace negotiations and revert to inflicting raw, naked, brutal force on the Palestinians. At that time, I had been invited by my colleague and friend, Professor Jamal Nassar, a Palestinian American, Chair of the Political Science Department at Illinois State University, to give a public lecture on this whole series of events. At the end of this lecture, which was dated 30 November 2000, I publicly issued a call for the establishment of an international campaign of divestment and disinvestment against Israel, on the same grounds that we had a campaign of divestment and disinvestment against the criminal apartheid regime in South Africa. I had been intimately involved in that campaign going back to my days as a student at Harvard Law School and had been involved in defending large numbers, sometimes successfully, of anti-apartheid protest cases in the United States. If you're interested you can read about those in my book, *Defending Civil Resistance Under International Law.*

I called for this campaign for the same reasons: Israel set up and has established an apartheid regime for the Palestinians, not only in occupied Palestine but also has treated their own Palestinians as third class citizens. And so the remedy must be the same: divestment/disinvestment.

The Cowardice of Harvard's Lawrence Summers

I'm not going to go through the subsequent history of the divestment/disinvestment movement[5] except to say that in the late summer of 2002 the President of Harvard, Larry Summers, accused those of us Harvard alumni involved in the Harvard divestment campaign of being anti-Semitic. After he made these charges, WBUR Radio Station in Boston, which is a National Public Radio affiliate, called me up and said: "We would like you to debate Summers for one hour on these charges, live." And I said, "I'd be happy to do so." They then called up Summers and he refused to debate me. Summers did not have the courage, the integrity, or the principles to back up his scurrilous charge. Eventually Harvard fired Summers because of his attempt to impose his Neo-Conservative agenda on Harvard, and in particular his other scurrilous charge that women are dumber than men when it comes to math and science. Well as a triple Harvard alumnus I say: Good riddance to Larry Summers! [laughter].

Debating Dershowitz

WBUR then called me back and said, "Well, since Summers won't debate you, would you debate Alan Dershowitz?" And I said, "Sure." So we had a debate for one hour, live on the radio. And there is a link that you can hear this debate if you want to. I still think it's the best debate out there on this whole issue of Israeli apartheid. Again, that would be WBUR Radio Station, Boston, 25 September 2002.

The problem with the debate, of course, is that Dershowitz knows nothing about international law and human rights. So he immediately started out by saying "well, there's no similarity between the apartheid regime in South Africa and what Israel is doing to the Palestinians." Well the problem with that is that Dershowitz did not know anything at all about even the existence of the Apartheid Convention. That is our second Handout for tonight. [*See* Handout 2, reprinted below.]

The definition of apartheid is set out in the Apartheid Convention of 1973. And this is taken from my book *Defending Civil Resistance Under International Law*—"Trial Materials on South Africa," published in 1987, that we used successfully to defend anti-apartheid resisters in the United States. If you take a look at the definition of apartheid found in Article 2, you will see that Israel has inflicted each and every act of apartheid set out in Article 2 on the Palestinians, except an outright ban on marriages between Israelis and Palestinians. But even there they have barred Palestinians living in occupied Palestine who marry Israeli citizens from moving into Israel, and thus defeat the right of family reunification that of course the world supported when Jews were emigrating from the Soviet Union.

Israel: An Apartheid State

Again, you don't have to take my word for it. There's an excellent essay today on *Counterpunch.org* by a leading Israeli human rights advocate, Shulamit Aloni, saying basically: "Yes we have an apartheid state in Israel."[6] Indeed, there are roads in the West Bank for Jews only. Palestinians can't ride there and now they're introducing new legislation that Jews cannot even drive on these roads with Palestinians in their cars.

This led my colleague and friend, Professor John Dugard, who is the U.N. Special Rapporteur for human rights in Palestine, to write an essay earlier this fall that you can get on Google, saying that in fact Israeli apartheid against the Palestinians is worse than the apartheid that the Afrikaners inflicted on the Blacks in South Africa.[7] Professor Dugard should know. He was one of a handful of courageous white international lawyers living in South Africa at the time who publicly and internationally condemned apartheid against Blacks at risk to his own life. Indeed, when I was litigating anti-apartheid cases on South Africa, we used Professor Dugard's book on *Human Rights and the South African Legal Order* as the definitive work explaining what apartheid is all about.

So Professor Dugard has recently made this statement. Of course President Carter has recently made this statement in his book too—that Israel is an apartheid state.[8] And certainly if you look at that definition of the Apartheid Convention, right there in front of you, it's clear—there are objective criteria. Indeed, if you read my *Palestinian* book, I have a Bibliography at the end with the facts right there, based on reputable human rights reports, Amnesty International, Human Rights Watch, etc. Many of them were also compiled and discussed by my friend Professor Norman Finklestein in his book *Beyond Chutzpah*, which I'd encourage you to read.

Israeli Apartheid: A Crime Against Humanity*

Article One of the Apartheid Convention defines apartheid as "a crime against humanity." Now Canada is not a party to the Apartheid Convention. However, there are 107 states parties that are. Canada is not and the United States is not. Why? Because both Canada and the United States are afraid that if they became parties to the Apartheid Convention, North American Indians would use the Apartheid Convention against them.

But Canada is a party to Rome Statute on the International Criminal Court, and the Rome Statute of the International Criminal Court clearly defines apartheid as a "crime against humanity." So even in a treaty to which Canada is a party, Canada recognizes apartheid as an international crime and a "crime against humanity." And that's Article 7 of the Rome Statute to which Canada is a party, paragraph 1, subparagraph j, "crime against humanity." The "crime of apartheid" is further defined in paragraph 2(h) as "inhumane acts of a character similar to those referred to in paragraph 1, committed in the context of an institutionalized regime of systematic oppression and domination by one racial group over any other racial group or groups and committed with the intention of maintaining that regime." Now that's Canadian law today. That's a treaty your own country has signed, under which apartheid is justiciable.

Giving the Palestinians Negotiating Leverage

All that being said then, tonight I would ask you people here at McMaster University to set up your own chapter of the Israeli divestment/disinvestment campaign that has taken off all over the United States and to join this worldwide movement of divestment/disinvestment. The Palestinians have no leverage in these negotiations. It's exactly the asymmetrical situation that Bertrand Russell pointed out in 1970 of an imperial power against a colonized power, as I can testify by my personal experience as one involved in these negotiations. It's very important, the insight here that Russell had, basically predicting the next 37 years or so of Israeli-Palestinian relations.

---

* *See also* Article 85(4)(c) of Additional Protocol I of 1977 to the Four Geneva Conventions of 1949 that defines apartheid as a "grave breach" thereof and thus a serious war crime for which there exists universal jurisdiction to prosecute offenders by any state in the world.

Join the divestment and disinvestment campaign, set up a chapter. It will take time. I remember when I came to the University of Illinois in 1978, we had our own divestment/disinvestment chapter on South Africa that I worked with and through large amounts of struggle, with even the University prosecuting students for a protest, most of whom we got off. But eventually the University of Illinois Board of Trustees divested. Unfortunately, Harvard only selectively divested but they selectively divested. I think as we saw in the South African divestment and disinvestment campaign—certainly in the United States, Canada, Europe—divestment had a very important role to play in bringing about the end of apartheid in South Africa. I personally think and submit that we can do the same here.

Go For the Money!

So if you're asking: "What can be done? How can we do it?" go back and study what your predecessors did in opposing apartheid in South Africa and do the exact same thing* with respect to Israel. It might take six, seven, eight years, I don't know, I can't predict. But eventually I believe it will work. Because the bottom line is money. It's that simple. You're going after their money and that's something everyone can understand. That's ultimately something the Afrikaner apartheid regime in South Africa understood—going after their money—and finally they released Nelson Mandela and there were good faith negotiations. The criminal apartheid regime in South Africa was dismantled. The bantustans were ended. Today South Africa is a beacon of hope and reconciliation for people around the world. I believe the same is possible for Israel and Palestine, but they're not going to do it by themselves. The United States government is not going to do it. It's up to you and to me to do it. Thank you.

[Applause]

---

* On November 22, 2007 the First Palestinian Conference for the Boycott of Israel issued its Summary Report from Ramallah, Palestine in support of the global campaign for Boycott, Divestment, and Sanctions (BDS) against the Israeli criminal apartheid regime. **This seminal document definitively refutes the argument that the world should not support BDS because the campaign might harm the Palestinians. As this document proves, Palestinian civil society fully supports universalizing BDS as a non-violent form of civil resistance against Israel's criminal apartheid regime no matter what the cost to themselves.** This is similar to the calls two decades ago by Black South Africans to support first the Sullivan Principles and then the original Divestment/Disinvestment Campaign in order to peacefully dismantle the Afrikaner

QUESTIONS AND ANSWERS

MacQueen: Thank you, Professor Boyle. Our speaker has agreed to take questions so we can have some discussion. I believe that since he's had a busy schedule, I will restrict it to half an hour. And I will also chair this session. So I will recognize you and we'll go on from there. I ask only that you keep your questions as succinct as possible so that other people will have a chance to ask questions too. Yes, sir.

Uniting for Peace Resolution

Audience Member: My question was regarding one of the resolutions of the United Nations General Assembly. It is also known as the Uniting for Peace Resolution, number 377. And it was pretty famous. It was brought about by the United States against the Soviet Union and what the resolution actually does or says is, it somehow overrules the veto power of the five permanent members of the Security Council. My question is why didn't the P.L.O., when you were working with them, ever use this resolution against Israel?

Boyle: In fact they have. I did the memorandum for them. You can read it in my book *Palestine, Palestinians, and International Law*. I fully explained to the P.L.O. the meaning, significance and use of the Uniting for Peace Resolution. It was my idea. They have now invoked it about sixteen times. The last time was in reaction to the Israel aggression against Palestine this summer [2006].

The United Nations General Assembly has now for the first time ever set up a special committee to investigate Israeli crimes against Palestinians. *For the first time ever*. So they are incrementally using the Uniting for Peace Resolution. The General Assembly has also adopted a resolution recommending that all U.N. member states reject any goods, or commerce, or investment dealing with Israeli settlements on the West Bank and Gaza. So there are two of these resolutions adopted now that have operative significance.

This will take time. Obviously they have to consult. They have to get support. First, among the Arab block. Then they reach out to the broader non-aligned movement and they're moving step-by-step. In my

---

criminal apartheid regime—which is exactly what happened. History is repeating itself, and hopefully with the same results for Palestinians and Israelis. Someday in my lifetime the Republic of Palestine and the Republic of Israel can become beacons of Hope for all humankind. Free Palestine! Boycott Israel!

opinion they're doing the best they can. Remember the mightiest power in the world is fighting them every step of the way—the United States.

I know many of you are Palestinians and you've probably have been very critical of President Arafat. The late Edward Said was my good friend and he said some things pretty critical of President Arafat as well and I very well might agree with some of them. But if you look at what they're up against—it's enormous power. They're making the best use of the law and diplomacy that they can. But this is a very significant breakthrough, now. They invoked Uniting for Peace again this summer [2006] to get the General Assembly to set up the committee to investigate these crimes. I have not talked recently with their new U.N. Ambassador, but I'm sure they will build on that, and that's the way they have to go.

The Essence of Palestinian Sovereignty

They have to go one step at a time. They can't go for the big enchilada. It has to be slow. This problem has been around for a hundred years, it's not going to be solved tomorrow. But it's important to remember what the late, great Yale Law Professor Myres McDougal, a friend of mine, said. I gave a lecture once at Yale Law School on the creation of the Palestinian state. Professor McDougal honored me by attending and he publicly said to me there: "Francis, just remember the strongest argument you have is that your people are still living on their own land and they are asserting their rights." That's the essence of sovereignty. A people living on their own land and asserting their rights and asserting their statehood.

The Two-State Solution

While the United States government still refuses to recognize the Palestinian state, the rest of the world does. The United Nations does. They would admit the Palestinian state if not for the U.S. veto. I guess Canada doesn't recognize the Palestinian state, but most of the rest of the world does. At one point, there were more states with diplomatic relations with Palestine than there were with Israel, not that at the end of the day that should mean anything.

We should have two states, both with U.N. membership, working as equals and negotiating as equals, and not in an imperial/colonial context as identified by Russell back in 1970. He fit the struggle within the context of imperialism and colonialism, which I think is correct. Well South Africa was an imperial-colonial state too, and eventually the South Africans worked it out. But again, given the political dynamics here the Palestinians are going to need help as the Blacks in South Africa needed help. A lot of money goes from the United States to Israel; goes from Canada to Israel. So you have influence here, but you have to get organized.

South African Apartheid Versus Israeli Apartheid

Audience Member: You have suggested here that if we use the same approach that was used with South Africa, that we can reach a solution eventually. But it seems to me that there is a big difference in the influence that Israel exerts on U.S. politics that is not matched in any way, that it is much higher than the influence that South Africa had on the politics in the U.K. or in the U.S. So if something was achieved in ten years with the South African regime it could take up to a hundred to two hundred years with the U.S. supporting the Israeli regime. I would request for you to comment.

Grassroots Movement for the Palestinians

Boyle: Sure. Well first I don't think it will. The Palestinians have never had a grassroots movement to support them in the United States until I called for the formation of the divestment/disinvestment campaign. And that was at the end of November 2000. In the United States—I can't speak for Canada, but certainly in the United States—the only progressive change we have ever seen has come from the people and grassroots movements. It has never come from the Presidency or the executive branch, it has never come from Congress. Whether it was civil rights for Black people; opposing the Vietnam war, which Russell again was in the vanguard of, not in America, but internationally; the nuclear freeze movement; or terminating the criminal aggression against Nicaragua by the Reagan administration. None of that would have happened without a grassroots movement. Finally we now have a grassroots movement among common, ordinary everyday Americans in support of the Palestinians. So that is very important.

Support for South African Apartheid in the United States

Second, there actually was enormous support for apartheid

South Africa in the United States. Apartheid South Africa was considered a key ally, a de facto ally, in the so-called fight against Communism, for control and domination of sub-Saharan Africa, for transportation of ships across the Horn, and for strategic minerals. So the United States fully, unequivocally supported the apartheid regime from the time when it was set up by Vorster, until the presidency of Jimmy Carter. He was the only exception, the only president who opposed apartheid. And then Reagan again right after fully supported the apartheid regime. He even had Mandela put on the U.S. terrorist watch list. And by the way, I'm on the U.S. government's terrorist watch list—I kid you not, I'm there, I'm on it [laughter]. And it's a nice list to be on. I'm happy to be on the same list as Mandela [applause].

The South African Divestment Campaign

So all of Washington, the elite of the country, fully supported that regime. And there were enormous investments in South Africa as you correctly pointed out—by Britain and also by the United States. In the United States, Randall Robertson, a graduate of the Harvard Law School, a little ahead of me, set this movement up, facing incredible odds. The apartheid regime in South Africa went out and hired the top law firms and lobbying firms in the country to oppose this movement. I was up against some of them. But eventually it was the common, ordinary, decent people of America who organized. Who finally said, "Enough is enough," and pressured the government to do the right thing. So I'm not as pessimistic as you might be; we faced incredible odds.

I remember the early days getting involved in this and it seemed almost impossible, as if we were Don Quixotes tilting at windmills but eventually that regime collapsed. It could not withstand the light of day. It could not withstand the truth. I do not believe that what Israel is doing to the Palestinians can stand the light of day either. So it was a ferocious battle against apartheid in South Africa, and it will be a ferocious battle against the apartheid regime in Israel. It might take a little longer, I don't know. But what alternative do we have? If we want to see peace in the Middle East we have to move in that direction. Otherwise things could get a lot worse.

Divvying Up Palestinian Land

Audience Member: Most recently we heard that Israel offered the Palestinians 95% of the land and the Israelis only wanted to take 5% at the Camp David II negotiations. And that logic it's like having somebody on the roof there with a gun sitting in a two foot saying, "Well we offered them 95% of the land why don't they accept that?" Any reasonable person would say, "Well, that's stupid not to accept it" but they don't say: what is it, that 5%, that they want to try to take off?

All these walls between urban areas of Palestine. It's terrifying. I don't know maybe this is a different question, but I don't know whether the United States is really interested in creating a peaceful Middle East. My fear is they suspect that having an independent Middle East is going to give Middle Eastern people control over their oil and this is what the Americans will not give up.

Boyle: Well on your first point of course I agree with you. That's exactly what Russell said here in this statement, right: "This is the traditional role of the imperial power, because it wishes to consolidate with the least difficulty what it has already taken by violence. Every new conquest becomes the new basis of the proposed negotiation from strength, which ignores the injustice of the previous aggression." That's exactly what Israel's negotiations are all about. That's right. So you're right.

Education Against Apartheid

The divestment/disinvestment campaign on South Africa—taking your case out to the people, not targeting government elites, but taking your case out to the people—must also have an educational component. Most people don't know anything about the plight of the Palestinians. They didn't know anything about apartheid in South Africa until we educated them and then they learned. So I too believe that there must be an educational component. I take it they're making a video of this tonight. You have my permission to do what you want with that video. Put it on cable TV, give it to CBC, do whatever you think you can do, but you're going to have to educate people, as we did on apartheid in South Africa and eventually that did work.

The Neo-Cons Are Neo-Nazis

Now your second point about the United States. Sure, the government of the United States, however, is very different from the American people. As I'm sure it's the case here in Canada especially now with Mr. Harper in power, right? I've read some of the statements made by Mr. Harper. I guess he's a soul mate of President Bush. I'll be talking about impeaching President Bush tomorrow night.

But, yes, to address the current constellation of people running the United States government, the Neo-Conservatives. I went to the University of Chicago with many of them. I was trained by the Straussians. Strauss had retired when I arrived but I was educated by his foremost student, protégé and literary executor, Joseph Cropsey. Wolfowitz was there, Khalilzad, Shulsky, were there, all the Neo-Cons were there when I was there. I went through the exact same program.

Leo Strauss's mentor in Germany before he immigrated to the United States was Carl Schmitt who later went on to become the most notorious law professor of the Nazi era. He legally justified, or tried to, every hideous atrocity the Nazis inflicted on anyone. Similarly, in the United States, there are lawyers like Dershowitz, Professor Yoo at Berkeley, now also Professor Goldsmith at Harvard Law School, who have publicly advocated torture. Despite my best efforts the Neo-Conservative Harvard Law School hired Goldsmith, a torture lawyer and war criminal, and he's now on the faculty with Dershowitz. They now have five Professors of Law at least at the Harvard Law School who publicly advocate torture.[9] That's the mentality of the people we're dealing with. The Neo-Cons are Neo-Nazis, and they're the ones running the White House today.

So with the rest of the American people, we're doing the best that we can. But you have to distinguish the government from the people. That was the beauty of the original divestment/disinvestment campaign—taking the case out to the people. I suspect that would be the beauty here in Canada. Again I haven't lived up here but I've come up here many times and lectured. Actually I think it would be a lot easier probably here in Canada than in the United States. But right now I think you're right.

The United States as a Dishonest Broker[10]

It's clear the Israeli massacres last summer [2006] against Lebanon and Palestine had the green light from the Neo-Cons in the White House. If we cannot stop them in the United States they very well might induce our government to attack Iran and Syria as well. That's a very serious danger. These people are fanatics, they are Neo-Nazis. The Deputy National Security Advisor in the White House running all this in the Middle East is Elliot Abrams, my classmate at Harvard Law School. Elliot Abrams bears responsibility for the murder of 35,000 people in Nicaragua. He ran that *contra*-war for Reagan. He willingly promoted activities that led to the murder of 35,000 people. I was down there in the war zone in 1985 investigating *contra* atrocities with two French Canadian human rights lawyers, Ramsey Clark, a previous Bertrand Russell lecturer, and Len Weinglass. We saw what Elliot Abrams did. Well now he's back, this Neo-Con war criminal, and fanatical Likudnik. And he's running the whole show now for Bush. So you're right. But again you're wasting your time talking to them. Their minds are made up. You have to take your case out to the people. That's the only hope we have.

Caterpillar Is the Worst Offender

Audience Member: Yes, could you give us a little more information about the project involving divestment and disinvestment and what kind of companies would be on the list? Thank you.

Boyle: Right. The first student organization to take up my call for setting up divestment/disinvestment was the Students for Justice in Palestine at the University of California, Berkeley—not surprisingly, Berkeley being in the vanguard. They have a web page, and on the web page they list the corporations. So there's a very extensive list, you can take your choice. Some have picked out Caterpillar, Rachel Corrie being murdered by a Caterpillar tractor. They are going after Caterpillar. Well there's a huge list; you're going to have to engage in some degree of selectivity. But Caterpillar's one of the worse and they're right near where I live in Peoria, Illinois. So there are priorities. The investment mix might differ up here in Canada, I don't know. But there is a list and you can find it there at their web page. Caterpillar is one of the worst.

Support for Yesh Gvul and Israeli Military Resisters

Audience Member: Ok. I just wanted to mention that there is an organized boycott at this point of Indigo/Chapter books that people here should know about. The owner of Indigo here in Canada is someone called Heather Riceman and she is partnered with Jerry Schwartz. And the two of them are quite involved in the Israeli state on many levels. One is Jerry Schwartz is part of, is quite involved in military weapons and also involved in Hessac which is an organization to support old soldiers in the IDF in Israel as well. So there is an organized boycott happening here and I put this to the audience to think about boycotting Indigo/Chapters.

Boyle: Yes, I've read about that, I think that that's important. Indeed what we should be doing is supporting Israeli soldiers who refuse as a matter of principle to serve on the West Bank and there are many of them. They have an organization called Yesh Gvul. I've been a member for years of Friends of the Yesh Gvul, founded by a friend of mine, Doron Vilner. We need to support these people. Very little is said about them, indeed most of that is just knocked out of the news media. So there are very courageous people over there in Israel, up against the wall and fighting this battle. Like Professor Dugard did in South Africa. We need to support them and give them support financially, morally, politically, whatever we can do.

Apartheid in South Africa and Israel

If you are interested in more of the background on the divestment/disinvestment campaign against South Africa, I have an entire chapter, I would say seventy pages, in this book *Defending Civil Resistance* that you can get at Amazon.com for $10. Anyone, even a student can afford ten dollars, right? You just forego a couple beers or cappuccinos (laughter). And you can see that battle and struggle against apartheid in South Africa and the legal principles we used to successfully pull that off and apply them here, because the principles are the same. It's the Apartheid Convention. Again Dershowitz really had nothing to say. Indeed, eventually he said, "Well, you are the expert on human rights." That was nice to get that concession from him. But now I encourage you to hear that debate because you have two Harvard trained lawyers arguing this precise issue. And now there's more media attention. President Carter said Israel is an apartheid state. Well, ok, but he isn't a lawyer. So you have Dershowitz against me. I'd encourage you to listen to that debate and draw your own conclusions.

Lessons from the South African Divestment/Disinvestment Campaign

Audience Member: Thank you Graeme. Many years ago, right here on the campus of McMaster University, I had the pleasure of participating in shutting down the meeting of the Senate of the University when it refused to endorse a motion to divest itself from investments in South Africa. And as a result of that, there was a student occupation on some of the premises of the University. And if I remember correctly, the University eventually did divest from its investments in South Africa. It was a small event on the world scale, but it was part of a world movement to beat apartheid. And I hope that the students of today at McMaster University will take a lead from Mr. Boyle's speech and carry on the fight and force McMaster University to divest itself of its interests in apartheid in Israel. I do have a couple of questions.

Audience Member: On March 17 around the world there will be demonstrations on the 4th anniversary of the invasion of Iraq by the United States and England. And there will be one in Hamilton as well. It will also be against the occupation of Iraq, against the occupation of Afghanistan and against the occupation of the West Bank and Gaza. So I'm hoping people will attend. That's at 1 P.M. on March 17, in front of Hamilton City Hall. The question is this: some people have rejected the two states solution for Israel and Palestine. And I'm talking about a one-state bi-national solution for the problem. I wondered what your opinion was on that.

Boyle: Yes. So on your first point on the South African divestment/ disinvestment campaign here at McMaster that was successful, and I'm very glad to hear it. We were successful at the University of Illinois. Although three students got convicted. They didn't serve time, but they paid a price. The rest, we got off. As I said, Harvard didn't divest completely despite our best efforts. But what it shows is that we're not reinventing the wheel here. We're just doing the same thing because the problem is the same: apartheid. So what I would encourage you students to do, go back in the archives of the *Silhouette*.[11] Research what the students did here back in the 1980s, and then look at the tactics and the strategy that succeeded. Then obviously you'll have to change them, modify them or whatever, but that's your road map.

A One-State Solution?

Now on the second point there is a long history here on the one-state solution that I'm not going to go over since we're running late. For the Partition Resolution, the original U.N. report had two solutions. The first was the majority report: two states with an international trusteeship for Jerusalem. The minority report was one-state, a federal state. Now I've reviewed the history here of the Palestinians accepting the two-state position. My feeling, for what it's worth, just looking at it from the Palestinian perspective is: Why should they give up the state they already have?

Now I know my friend Ali Abunima, who is a Palestinian

American graduate of the University of Chicago, Ph.D. in Middle East Studies where I went, has written a very fine book on this point.[12]

I'd encourage you to read it, but I would respectfully disagree. The leadership of the Palestinian people acting pursuant to my advice, the P.L.O. and the Palestine National Council that speaks for all Palestinians all over the world, have accepted a two-state solution. This took a lot of work and that has been their official position since 1988. I do not detect any sentiment, certainly among Palestinians living in Palestine, for one-state. Likewise, there might be a handful of Israelis who would opt for a one-state solution, I don't know. But two-states is their official position as well. I don't really see a one-state solution right now as getting anywhere, with all due respect to Dr. Abunimah.

One-State In the Future?

Perhaps it could be that thirty years from now when the Palestinian state has been up and operating and independent, and the Palestinians have shook off the Israeli colonial occupation, and a new generation of Palestinians and Israelis say to each other, "well, this is a small land maybe we should come together," I don't know. But it's not to preclude that a generation or two from now. I'm not ruling it out. Indeed, now if Israeli leaders and the Palestinians were to instruct me to draw up a one-state proposal, I would do it. But that's not the current position. So I don't really see that getting anywhere.

But I do go back to my first point, hey, the Palestinian state is recognized by 130 states. Maybe it isn't recognized by Canada but it's recognized by 130 states. We have de facto membership in the United Nations. Why should we give any of that up now?

Finally, the entire international grassroots Movement calling for Boycott, Divestment, and Sanctions (BDS) against Israel is founded upon the objective of achieving a two-state solution. For us to move over to advocating one state at this time would literally pull the rug out from under the BDS Movement, which is one of the most effective external sources of hope and help that the Palestinians have in the world today. We must do nothing to jeopardize the worldwide BDS Movement. We must keep hope alive for the Palestinians—and the Israelis.

Conclusion

MacQueen: I know there are many more questions that people would like to ask but our half hour is over and my job is to protect the speaker from exhaustion. I'm sure if there's a burning question you have to ask you can come up and do so in a moment. I just wanted to say that I believe Mark Vorobej at the McMaster Bookstore has a display of Professor Boyle's books. So I encourage you to go to McMaster Bookstore and have a look around, and buy the ones you wish, and that will allow you to follow up on some of the ideas you've heard tonight. Having said that then I would like to ask Joanna Santa-Barbara to offer thanks to our speaker.

Santa-Barbara: It's an honor to thank you, Professor Boyle, for an evening that has been quite outstanding for its clarity of exposition. But far more, I think, than a wonderfully clear and knowledgeable presentation; I think that what we have heard beneath that is enormous compassion for people who are in a position of being under the odds. Whether persons, or nations, if there's an underdog, whether it's an obscure person claiming conscientious objection status, a nation up against a super-power, or in fact all of us under the constant threat of nuclear weapons in the hands of the powerful, it would seem that Professor Boyle will be there on the scene [laughter].

I want to thank you for the application of your brilliant knowledge, and your practice of international law and as we can understand it: the real love of law and justice to protect all. For the intense, passionate determination to use the law for one of what I think is one of its most magnificent purposes—to constrain the powerful and protect the powerless. And for Professor Boyle's tremendous courage to stand against the mainstream at considerable cost, potentially to issues of career, even to life. The courage to criticize wrongdoing in high places. I think of Professor Boyle as that child in the crowd who said, "Look, the emperor has no clothes." And finally, I thank you for giving us more than a brilliant intellectual analysis—for giving us a call to action. Thank you.

[Grand Applause!]

Lord Russell's Last Message

This statement on the Middle East is dated 31st January, 1970, and was read on 3rd February, the day after Russell's death, to an International Conference of Parliamentarians meeting in Cairo.

The latest phase of the undeclared war in the Middle East is based upon a profound miscalculation. The bombing raids deep into Egyptian territory will not persuade the civilian population to surrender, but will stiffen their resolve to resist. This is the lesson of all aerial bombardment. The Vietnamese, who have endured years of American heavy bombing, have responded not by capitulation but by shooting down more enemy aircraft. In 1940 my own fellow countrymen resisted Hitler's bombing raids with unprecedented unity and determination. For this reason, the present Israeli attacks will fail in their essential purpose, but at the same time they must be condemned vigorously throughout the world.

The development of the crisis in the Middle East is both dangerous and instructive. For over 20 years Israel has expanded by force of arms. After every stage in this expansion Israel has appealed to "reason" and has suggested "negotiations." This is the traditional role of the imperial power, because it wishes to consolidate with the least difficulty what it has already taken by violence. Every new conquest becomes the new basis of the proposed negotiation from strength, which ignores the injustice of the previous aggression. The aggression committed by Israel must be condemned, not only because no state has the right to annex foreign territory, but because every expansion is an experiment to discover how much more aggression the world will tolerate.

The refugees who surround Palestine in their hundreds of thousands were described recently by the Washington journalist I.F. Stone as "the moral millstone around the neck of world Jewry." Many of the refugees are now well into the third decade of their precarious existence in temporary settlements. The tragedy of the people of Palestine is that their country was "given" by a foreign Power to another people for the creation of a new State. The result was that many hundreds of thousands of innocent people were made permanently homeless. With every new conflict their numbers have increased. How much longer is the world willing to endure this spectacle of wanton cruelty? It is abundantly clear that the refugees have every right to the homeland from which they were driven, and the denial of this right is at the heart of the continuing conflict. No people anywhere in the world would accept being expelled en masse from their own country; how can anyone require the people of Palestine to accept a punishment which nobody else would tolerate? A permanent just settlement of the refugees in their homeland is an essential ingredient of any genuine settlement in the Middle East.

We are frequently told that we must sympathize with Israel because of the suffering of the Jews in Europe at the hands of the Nazis. I see in this suggestion no reason to perpetuate any suffering. What Israel is doing today cannot be condoned, and to invoke the horrors of the past to justify those of the present is gross hypocrisy. Not only does Israel condemn a vast number of refugees to misery; not only are many Arabs under occupation condemned to military rule; but also Israel condemns the Arab nations only recently emerging from colonial status, to continued impoverishment as military demands take precedence over national development.

All who want to see an end to bloodshed in the Middle East must ensure that any settlement does not contain the seeds of future conflict. Justice requires that the first step towards a settlement must be an Israeli withdrawal from the territories occupied in June, 1967. A new world campaign is needed to help bring justice to the long-suffering people of the Middle East.

HANDOUT 2
Excerpts from the Convention on Apartheid

The system of apartheid has been made criminal by the International Convention on the Suppression and Punishment of the Crime of Apartheid, General Assembly Resolution 3068(XXVIII) (1973), which provides in pertinent part:

Article I

1. The States Parties to the present Convention declare that apartheid is a crime against humanity and that inhuman acts resulting from the policies and practices of apartheid and similar policies and practices of racial segregation and discrimination, as defined in Article II of the Convention, are crimes violating the principles of international law, in particular the purposes and principles of the Charter of the United Nations, and constituting a serious threat to international peace and security.

2. The States Parties to the present Convention declare

criminal those organizations, institutions and individuals committing the crime of apartheid.

Article II

For the purposes of the present Convention, the term "the crime of apartheid," which shall include similar policies and practices of racial segregation and discrimination as practiced in southern Africa, shall apply to the following inhuman acts committed for the purpose of establishing and maintaining domination by one racial group of persons over any other racial group of persons and systematically oppressing them:

(a) Denial to a member or members of a racial group or groups of the right to life and liberty of person:

(i) By murder of members of a racial group or groups;

(ii) By the infliction upon the members of a racial group or groups of serious bodily or mental harm, by the infringement of their freedom or dignity, or by subjecting them to torture or to cruel, inhuman or degrading treatment or punishment;

(iii) By arbitrary arrest and illegal imprisonment of the members of a racial group or groups;

(b) Deliberate imposition on a racial group or groups of living conditions calculated to cause its or their physical destruction in whole or in part;

(c) Any legislative measures and other measures calculated to prevent a racial group or groups from participation in the political, social, economic and cultural life of the country and the deliberate creation of conditions preventing the full development of such a group or groups, in particular by denying to members of a racial group or groups basic human rights and freedoms, including the right to work, the right to form recognized trade unions, the right to education, the right to leave and to return to their country, the right to a nationality, the right to freedom of movement and residence, the right to freedom of opinion and expression, and the right to freedom of peaceful assembly and association;

(d) Any measures, including legislative measures, designed to divide the population along racial lines by the creation of separate reserves and ghettos for the members of a racial group or groups, the prohibition of mixed marriages among members of various racial groups, the expropriation of landed property belonging to a racial group or groups or to members thereof;

(e) Exploitation of the labour of the members of a racial group or groups, in particular by submitting them to forced labour;

(f) Persecution of organizations and persons, by depriving them of fundamental rights and freedoms, because they oppose apartheid.

NOTES

[1]   The key U.S. State Department officials who dealt with the Middle East Peace negotiations were Dennis Ross, Edward Djerejian, Aaron Miller and Dan Kurtzer.

[2]   Hilde Henriksen Waage, *Norway's Role in the Middle East Peace Talks: Between a Strong State and a Weak Belligerent*, 34 J. Palestine Stud., No. 4, at 6-24 (Summer 2005).

[3]   Francis A. Boyle, Palestine, Palestinians, and International Law 78-118 (2003).

[4]   *Memorandum on the Yaron Case*, 5 Palestine Y.B. Int'l L. 254, 257 (1989).

[5]   *See* Palestine–Israel Action Group (PAIG), Subcommittee of the Peace and Social Concerns Committee of Ann Arbor (Michigan) Friends Meeting, Boycott, Divestment and Sanctions: An International Campaign on Behalf of Palestinian Human Rights and a Just and Viable Peace in Israel–Palestine—A Survey of Diverse Approaches to Ethical Economic Engagement Adopted by Groups and Individuals Worldwide (August 2007).

[6]   Shulamit Aloni, *Yes, There Is Apartheid in Israel,* Counterpunch.org, Jan. 8, 2007.

[7]   John Dugard, *Israelis Adopt What South Africa Dropped*, Atlanta Journal – Constitution, Nov. 29, 2006.

[8]   Jimmy Carter, Palestine: Peace Not Apartheid (2006).

[9]   Francis A. Boyle, *Harvard's Kangaroo Law School: The School for Torturers*, ZNET Magazine, June 10, 2007.

[10]   Naseer H. Aruri, Dishonest Broker (2003).

[11]   The student newspaper at McMaster University.

[12]   Ali Abunimah, One Country (2006).

APPENDIX 2

APPENDIX 2

TRYING TO STOP AGGRESSIVE WAR

AND GENOCIDE AGAINST

THE PEOPLE AND THE REPUBLIC

OF BOSNIA AND HERZEGOVINA

There are numerous accounts of the aggression and genocide perpetrated by the rump Yugoslavia and its Bosnian Serb surrogates against the People and the Republic of Bosnia and Herzegovina that have been written by journalists, historians, ambassadors, political scientists, and others. This paper tries to tell the story of Bosnia from the perspective of international law. The aggression and genocide against Bosnia and the refusal of the international community to stop it will prove to be one of the pivotal events of the post World War II era. This paper will try to explain what happened, why it happened, and, most importantly, what was wrong with what happened.

It is hoped that this analysis will prove useful to the People of Bosnia and Herzegovina as they struggle to reconstruct their lives and their State. Hopefully, a record of what happened in the past will provide the Bosnian People with a guide for the direction of their future. Concerning the utility of this study for the rest of the world, as George Santayana has said: "Those who cannot remember the past are condemned to repeat it."

On March 19, 1993, this author was appointed General Agent with Extraordinary and Plenipotentiary Powers "to institute, conduct and defend against any and all legal proceedings" for the Republic of Bosnia and Herzegovina before the International Court of Justice by His Excellency President Alija Izetbegovic while attending the so-called Vance-Owen negotiations in New York. The very next day the author instituted legal proceedings on behalf of the Republic of Bosnia and Herzegovina before the International Court of Justice in The Hague against the rump Yugoslavia for violating the 1948 Genocide Convention. On April 8, 1993, the author won an Order for provisional measures of protection from the World Court against the rump Yugoslavia that was overwhelmingly in favor of Bosnia and Herzegovina.

Generally put, the World Court ordered the rump Yugoslavia immediately to cease and desist from committing all acts of genocide in the Republic of Bosnia and Herzegovina, whether directly or indirectly by means of its surrogate Bosnian Serb military, paramilitary, and irregular armed units:

52. For these reasons,

The COURT,

Indicates, pending its final decision in the proceedings instituted on 20 March 1993 by the Republic of Bosnia and Herzegovina against the Federal Republic of Yugoslavia (Serbia and Montenegro), the following provisional measures:

A. (1) Unanimously,

The Government of the Federal Republic of Yugoslavia (Serbia and Montenegro) should immediately, in pursuance of its undertaking in the Convention on the Prevention and Punishment of the Crime of Genocide of 9 December 1948, take all measures within its power to prevent commission of the crime of genocide;

(2) By 13 votes to 1,

The Government of the Federal Republic of Yugoslavia (Serbia and Montenegro) should in particular ensure that any military, paramilitary or irregular armed units which may be directed or supported by it, as well as any organizations and persons which may be subject to its control, direction or influence, do not commit any acts of genocide, of conspiracy to commit genocide, of direct and public incitement to commit genocide, or of complicity in genocide, whether directed against the Muslim population of Bosnia and Herzegovina or against any other national, ethnical, racial or religious group;

IN FAVOUR: President Sir Robert Jennings; Vice-President Oda; Judges Ago, Schwebel, Bedjaoui,

Ni, Evensen, Guillaume, Shahabuddeen, Aguilar
Mawdsley, Weeramantry, Ranjeva, Ajibola;
AGAINST: Judge Tarassov;

B.   Unanimously,

The Government of the Federal Republic
of Yugoslavia (Serbia and Montenegro) and the
Government of the Republic of Bosnia and Herzegovina
should not take any action and should ensure that no
action is taken which may aggravate or extend the
existing dispute over the prevention or punishment
of the crime of genocide, or render it more difficult of
solution.

In his Declaration attached to the World Court's Order of 8 April
1993, the late Judge Tarassov from Russia provided a most authoritative
interpretation of Paragraph 52A(2) of the Court's Order:

...In my view, these passages of the Order are open
to the interpretation that the Court believes that the
Government of the Federal Republic of Yugoslavia
is indeed involved in such genocidal acts, or at least
that it may very well be so involved. Thus, on my view,
these provisions are very close to a pre-judgment of
the merits, despite the Court's recognition that, in an
Order indicating provisional measures, it is not entitled
to reach determinations of fact or law...

As I told the world's news media from the floor of the Great
Courtroom of the Peace Palace in The Hague immediately after the
close of the World Court's proceedings wherein this Order was handed
down, I fully agreed with Judge Tarassov in the following sense: This
Order was indeed a pre-judgment on the merits that genocide had been
inflicted by the rump Yugoslavia against the People and the Republic
of Bosnia and Herzegovina, both directly and indirectly by means of
its surrogates in the Bosnian Serb military, paramilitary, and irregular
armed units.

The unanimous ruling in Paragraph 52A(1) indicated that the
World Court believed there was more than enough evidence to conclude
that the rump Yugoslavia itself had inflicted genocide against the People
and the Republic of Bosnia and Herzegovina. The 13 to 1 ruling in
Paragraph 52A(2) indicated that the World Court believed there was

more than enough evidence to conclude that the rump Yugoslavia was legally responsible for the atrocities inflicted by the Bosnian Serb military, paramilitary, and irregular armed forces against the People and the Republic of Bosnia and Herzegovina. The 13 to 1 ruling in Paragraph 52A(2) also indicated that the World Court believed that there was more than enough evidence to conclude that these surrogate Bosnian Serb military, paramilitary, and irregular armed forces had inflicted acts of genocide, conspiracy to commit genocide, direct and public incitement to commit genocide, and complicity in genocide, against the People and the Republic of Bosnia and Herzegovina.

As the Lawyer for the entire Republic of Bosnia and Herzegovina and for all of its People, I had expressly asked the World Court to protect all of the national, ethnical, racial and religious groups in Bosnia from acts of genocide perpetrated by the rump Yugoslavia and by its surrogate Bosnian Serb military, paramilitary, and irregular armed forces, which the World Court did do in Paragraph 52A(2) of this Order. Of course, the first and foremost victims of this genocide were the Bosnian Muslims, but also came those Bosnian Croats, those Bosnian Serbs and those Bosnian Jews who supported the Republic of Bosnia and Herzegovina. However, most of the evidence of genocide that I submitted to the World Court concerned acts of genocide against Bosnia's Muslim population, to which the Bosnian Parliament awarded the name "Bosniaks." So the World Court went out of its way to protect by name "the Muslim population of Bosnia and Herzegovina" from acts of genocide by the surrogate Bosnian Serb military, paramilitary, and irregular armed forces in Paragraph 52A(2) of this 8 April 1993 Order.

Only the late Judge Tarassov from Russia objected to this express protection of Bosnian Muslims by name in his separate Declaration: "The lack of balance in these provisions is the clearer in view of the way in which the Court has singled out one element of the population of Bosnia and Herzegovina." Once again, I agree with Judge Tarassov in the sense that the overwhelming weight of the evidence did indeed call for the World Court to protect the Bosnian Muslims from genocide expressly by name. This entire World Court Order of 8 April 1993 was so completely unbalanced against the rump Yugoslavia and its surrogate Bosnian Serb military, paramilitary, and irregular armed forces because the evidence of their genocide against the People and the Republic of Bosnia and Herzegovina and, in particular, against the Bosnian Muslims, was so overwhelming.

The unanimous World Court ruling in Paragraph 52B was also a victory for the People and the Republic of Bosnia and Herzegovina. I had expressly asked the World Court to impose this protective measure upon both Bosnia and the rump Yugoslavia, which the Court did indeed do. My calculation was that the rump Yugoslavia would definitely violate this measure, whereas Bosnia would obey it. I felt it would be difficult to imagine how the victim of genocide could aggravate or extend the dispute over genocide with the perpetrator of genocide, or render that dispute more difficult of solution.

By voluntarily asking for the imposition of this measure upon both Bosnia and the rump Yugoslavia, I intended to entangle the rump Yugoslavia into a full-scale breach and open defiance of the most comprehensive World Court Order that I could obtain. This is exactly what happened. The rump Yugoslavia paid absolutely no attention whatsoever to the entirety of this 8 April 1993 Order. Whereas, by comparison, Bosnia obeyed this self-imposed requirement of Paragraph 52B not to aggravate or extend the dispute over genocide, or render it more difficult of a solution.

By means of obtaining the measure set forth in Paragraph 52B, *inter alia*, I intended to prepare the groundwork for harsher Security Council sanctions against the rump Yugoslavia. I also hoped to pave the way for a then already anticipated second round of provisional measures at the World Court in which I intended to expand the basis of my original Application/complaint against the rump Yugoslavia beyond the fixed parameters of the 1948 Genocide Convention. I needed to do that in order to break the genocidal arms embargo against Bosnia and also to stop the proposed racist carve-up of the Republic pursuant to the so-called Vance-Owen Plan, and then later, its successor, the genocidal Owen-Stoltenberg Plan.

By issuing this Order on 8 April 1993 the World Court necessarily and overwhelmingly rejected the bald-faced lies put forward by the rump Yugoslavia's Lawyer Shabtai Rosenne from Israel, that the bloodshed in Bosnia was the result of a civil war for which the rump Yugoslavia was in no way responsible. The World Court also overwhelmingly rejected Rosenne's argument that President Izetbegovic was not the lawful President of the Republic and therefore could not lawfully institute this lawsuit against the rump Yugoslavia and appoint me as Bosnia's Lawyer to argue this genocide case before the World Court. The World Court also overwhelmingly rejected Rosenne's request that provisional measures along the lines of those found in Paragraphs 52A(1) and (2) be imposed upon Bosnia because there was no evidence that the Government of the Republic of Bosnia and Herzegovina had committed genocide against anyone. Many of these so-called issues are still misrepresented by the rump Yugoslavia and its supporters around the world today despite the fact that they were decisively resolved by the World Court as long ago as 8 April 1993.

The World Court's Order of 8 April 1993 was an overwhelming and crushing defeat of the rump Yugoslavia by Bosnia on all counts save one: The World Court said nothing at all about the arms embargo, apparently because the Genocide Convention itself says nothing at all about the use of force to prevent genocide. Nevertheless, in this regard, the World Court did state quite clearly in Paragraph 45 of its 8 April 1993 Order that in accordance with the requirements of Article I of the Genocide Convention "...all parties to the Convention have thus undertaken 'to prevent and to punish' the crime of genocide..." The implication was quite clear that in the opinion of the World Court all 100+ states that were parties to the Genocide Convention had an absolute obligation "to prevent" the ongoing genocide against Bosnia. Therefore, although technically the World Court directed its 8 April 1993 Order against the rump Yugoslavia, the Court was telling every other state in the world community that each had an obligation "to prevent" the ongoing genocide against the People and the Republic of Bosnia and Herzegovina.

The World Court continued in Paragraph 45 with the following language: "...whereas in the view of the Court, in the circumstances brought to its attention and outlined above in which there is a *grave risk* of acts of genocide being committed..." (Emphasis added.) In other words, the World Court went as far as it could consistent with its Rules of Procedure toward definitively ruling that acts of genocide were actually being committed by the rump Yugoslavia and its surrogate Bosnian Serb armed forces against the People and the Republic of Bosnia and Herzegovina. At the time, this "grave risk of acts of genocide" language set forth in Paragraph 45 of the 8 April 1993 Order was as close as the World Court could go to rendering a pre-judgment on the merits of the dispute, as pointed out by the late Judge Tarassov in his Declaration.

Several hours after I had won this World Court Order for Bosnia, on 8 April 1993 the Clinton administration announced the imposition by NATO of a complete air interdiction zone above the Republic of Bosnia and Herzegovina whereby NATO jet fighters would shoot down any Serb jets, planes, and helicopters. The Serbs were no longer able to kill the Bosnians from the sky! Late that evening Hague time I was interviewed live by the BBC and asked to give my opinion on this so-called "no-fly zone" over Bosnia that was announced earlier in the day from Washington, D.C.: "...I certainly hope that the NATO pilots do not fly over Bosnia, watch the genocide, rape, murder, torture and killing go on, take pictures, send them back to NATO Headquarters, Washington, London and Paris, and then do nothing to stop it!" Yet, most tragically of all, that is exactly what happened until the Fall of 1995.

In accordance with its own terms, an original copy of this 8 April 1993 Order was transmitted "to the Secretary-General of the United Nations for transmission to the Security Council." In other words, the World Court officially informed the member states of the U.N. Security Council (1) that genocide was currently being inflicted by the rump Yugoslavia and its surrogate Bosnian Serb armed forces against the People and the Republic of Bosnia and Herzegovina; and also (2) that the member states of the Security Council had an absolute obligation under the Genocide Convention "to prevent" this ongoing genocide against Bosnia. According to Article 94(2) of the United Nations Charter, the Security Council is supposed to enforce such World Court Orders.

As I had anticipated, the rump Yugoslavia paid absolutely no attention whatsoever to the World Court's 8 April 1993 Order, and immediately proceeded to violate each and every one of its three provisional measures. But instead of punishing the rump Yugoslavia, the Security Council's Permanent Members—the United States, Britain, France, Russia, and China—decided to punish Bosnia, the victim, by imposing upon it the so-called Owen-Stoltenberg Plan as the successor to the Vance-Owen Plan, which had been rejected by the so-called Bosnian Serb Parliament. The Owen-Stoltenberg Plan would have carved-up the Republic of Bosnia and Herzegovina into three ethnically based mini-states, destroyed Bosnia's Statehood, and robbed Bosnia of its Membership in the United Nations Organization. Furthermore, in accordance with an internal study prepared by the United States Department of State, this proposed tripartite partition of Bosnia would have subjected approximately 1.5 to 2 million *more* Bosnians to "ethnic cleansing," which I had already argued to the World Court was a form of genocide.

Therefore, soon after my return from The Hague, the author set out to break the genocidal arms embargo against Bosnia and to stop this genocidal carve-up of the Republic of Bosnia and Herzegovina by drafting a Second Request for Provisional Measures of Protection to the International Court of Justice on behalf of Bosnia. Pursuant thereto, on July 26, 1993, the author spent the day at United Nations Headquarters in New York with Ambassador Muhamed Sacirbey of the Republic of Bosnia and Herzegovina, publicly briefing large numbers of Ambassadors, as well as privately briefing the Non-Aligned member states of the Security Council and the then President of the Council

Ambassador Diego Arias from Venezuela, about this Second Request to the International Court of Justice for an Interim Order of Protection on behalf of the Republic of Bosnia and Herzegovina. In that location and on that day, as Bosnia's Lawyer I publicly threatened to sue the Permanent Members of the Security Council over the arms embargo, with Ambassador Sacirbey sitting at my side. As I said at that time and place, the Security Council's arms embargo against the Republic of Bosnia and Herzegovina had aided and abetted genocide against the Bosnian People.

The five Permanent Members of the Security Council--United States, United Kingdom, Russia, France, China--bear special responsibility for aiding and abetting genocide against the People and the Republic of Bosnia and Herzegovina in violation of the 1948 Genocide Convention. I would have been happy to have sued the Permanent Members of the Security Council for Bosnia, and had offered to do so on more than one occasion to the Bosnian Presidency. The same condemnation can be applied as well to all those U.N. member states that had served on the Security Council from 1992 through 1995 and had routinely supported the continuation of this genocidal arms embargo against Bosnia.

That evening, the author flew to The Hague and filed this Second Request for Interim Protection at the World Court on 27 July 1993. The very next day, 28 July 1993, the author flew to Geneva in order to serve as the Legal Adviser to President Alija Izetbegovic, then Foreign Minister (later Prime Minister) Haris Silajdic,* and all of the Members of the collective Presidency of the Republic of Bosnia and Herzegovina during the so-called Owen-Stoltenberg negotiations. There I personally disrupted the Owen-Stoltenberg Plan to carve-up the Republic into three pieces, to destroy Bosnia's Statehood, and to rob Bosnia of its Membership in the United Nations Organization. In addition, President Izetbegovic had also instructed me to negotiate in good faith over the so-called "package" of proposed documents with David Owen and his lawyer Paul Szasz. The author served in that capacity until August 10, 1993, when the talks had broken down. The author then returned home in order to prepare for Bosnia's second oral argument before the World Court.

The author then argued the Second Request for provisional measures of protection for Bosnia and Herzegovina before the World Court on 25 and 26 August 1993. The author then won the Second Order of Provisional Protection on behalf of Bosnia from the World

---

*Later Bosnian President.

Court on 13 September 1993. Generally put, this second World Court Order demanded that the Court's first Order of 8 April 1993 "should be immediately and effectively implemented":

> 61. For these reasons,
> THE COURT
> (1) By 13 votes to 2,
> Reaffirms the provisional measure indicated in paragraph 52 A (1) of the Order made by the Court on 8 April 1993, which should be immediately and effectively implemented;

> IN FAVOUR: President Sir Robert Jennings; Vice-President Oda; Judges Schwebel, Bedjaoui, Ni, Evensen, Guillaume, Shahabuddeen, Aguilar Mawdsley, Weeramantry, Ajibola, Herczegh; Judge ad hoc Lauterpacht;
> AGAINST: Judge Tarassov; Judge ad hoc Kreca;

> (2) By 13 votes to 2,
> Reaffirms the provisional measure indicated in paragraph 52 A (2) of the Order made by the Court on 8 April 1993, which should be immediately and effectively implemented;

> IN FAVOUR: President Sir Robert Jennings; Vice-President Oda; Judges Schwebel, Bedjaoui, Ni, Evensen, Guillaume, Shahabuddeen, Aguilar Mawdsley, Weeramantry, Ajibola, Herczegh; Judge ad hoc Lauterpacht;
> AGAINST: Judge Tarassov; Judge ad hoc Kreca;

> (3) By 14 votes to 1,
> Reaffirms the provisional measure indicated in paragraph 52 B of the Order made by the Court on 8 April 1993, which should be immediately and effectively implemented.

> IN FAVOUR: President Sir Robert Jennings; Vice-President Oda; Judges Schwebel, Bedjaoui, Ni, Evensen, Tarassov, Guillaume, Shahabuddeen, Aguilar

Mawdsley, Weeramantry, Ajibola, Herczegh; Judge ad
hoc Lauterpacht;
AGAINST: Judge ad hoc Kreca.

In his Dissenting Opinion attached to this second World Court
Order of 13 September 1993, the late Judge Tarassov from Russia
once again provided a most authoritative interpretation of its meaning
and significance:

....

Given that requests for the indication of
provisional measures have been submitted by both
Parties in new proceedings and given the numerous
communications on which those requests are based,
regarding acts which allegedly relate to the crime of
genocide and which have purportedly been committed
in this inter-ethnic, civil conflict in Bosnia and
Herzegovina by all ethnic groups against each other,
the Court's decision to make an order ascribing the
lion's share of responsibility for the prevention of acts
of genocide in Bosnia and Herzegovina to Yugoslavia
is a one-sided approach based on preconceived ideas,
which borders on a pre-judgment of the merits of the
case and implies an unequal treatment of the different
ethnic groups in Bosnia and Herzegovina who have
all suffered inexpressibly in this fratricidal war. I, as a
judge, cannot support this approach. ...
....

...While the one-sided, unbalanced Order of
the Court might not necessarily be 'an obstacle to a
negotiated settlement,' it will obviously not facilitate its
successful completion. ...

Once again, I fully agreed with the late Judge Tarassov's
characterization of this second World Court Order of 13 September
1993 in the following sense:

It was indeed completely "one-sided" and "unbalanced" in favor
of Bosnia and against the rump Yugoslavia and its surrogate Bosnian
Serb armed forces. This second World Court Order clearly did ascribe
"the lion's share of responsibility" for the atrocities in Bosnia to the
rump Yugoslavia and its surrogate Bosnian Serb military, paramilitary,
and irregular armed forces. This second Order clearly represented a

"one-sided approach" by the World Court in favor of Bosnia against the rump Yugoslavia and its surrogate Bosnian Serb armed forces. Moreover, this second Order clearly accorded the Bosnian Muslims "unequal treatment" because of the Order's reaffirmation of their express protection by name. The World Court had indeed developed the "preconceived ideas" that the Bosnian Muslims were the primary victims of Serb genocide against the People and the Republic of Bosnia and Herzegovina precisely because of the overwhelming evidence I had submitted to that effect starting on 20 March 1993 when I originally filed the lawsuit. Finally, this second World Court Order of 13 September 1993 was even more of "a pre-judgment on the merits of the case" than was the first Order of 8 April 1993.

Immediately after the receipt of this second World Court Order, the Serb Ambassador sat down dejectedly in the Hall of the Peace Palace just outside the Great Courtroom and was asked by the world news media what he thought about the new Order: "It is even worse than the first one!" The world news media then asked me what I thought about his comment: "It is the first truthful statement they have ever made here at the World Court." You have to give the devil his due when he is telling the truth.

In order to render this second Order, the World Court once again necessarily and overwhelmingly rejected the bald-faced lies put forward by Rosenne and in addition now by three Serb lawyers who had joined him, that what was happening in Bosnia was a civil war for which the rump Yugoslavia bore no responsibility. Once again, the World Court overwhelmingly rejected Rosenne's argument that President Izetbegovic was not the legitimate President of the Republic of Bosnia and Herzegovina entitled to have me argue these proceedings before the World Court in his name and in the name of the Republic. Finally, the World Court once again overwhelmingly rejected the request by Rosenne to impose a proposed provisional measure against Bosnia along the lines of Paragraph 52A(1) of its 8 April 1993 Order because there was still no evidence that the Republic of Bosnia and Herzegovina had committed genocide against anyone.

This second World Court Order of 13 September 1993 was a crushing and overwhelming victory for Bosnia against the rump Yugoslavia on all counts but one: The World Court once again refused to say anything directly about the arms embargo, apparently because the Genocide Convention itself said nothing about the use of force to prevent genocide. Nevertheless, in Paragraph 50 of this second Order the World Court quoted verbatim Article I of the 1948 Genocide

Convention and then expressly held: "...whereas all parties to the Convention have thus undertaken to prevent and to punish the crime of genocide;..." Once again, the World Court was telling all 100+ states parties to the Genocide Convention that each had an obligation "to prevent" the ongoing genocide in Bosnia, and this time by means of the "immediate and effective implementation" of its 8 April 1993 Order as called for by Paragraph 59 of this second Order, inter alia, which will be quoted in full below.

These preliminary conclusions become perfectly clear by means of a detailed examination of the next several paragraphs of this second World Court Order of 13 September 1993:

> 51. Whereas, as the Court recorded in its Order of 8 April 1993, the crime of genocide "shocks the conscience of mankind, results in great losses to humanity ... and is contrary to moral law and to the spirit and aims of the United Nations," in the words of General Assembly resolution 96 (1) of 11 December 1946 on "The Crime of Genocide";

> 52. Whereas, since the Order of 8 April 1993 was made, and despite that Order, and despite many resolutions of the Security Council of the United Nations, great suffering and loss of life has been sustained by the population of Bosnia-Herzegovina in circumstances which shock the conscience of mankind and flagrantly conflict with moral law and the spirit and aims of the United Nations;...

In accordance with its own Rules of Procedure, during the two provisional measures phases of these proceedings the World Court could not technically render a final Judgment on the merits that the rump Yugoslavia and its surrogate Bosnian Serb armed forces had committed acts of "genocide" against the People and the Republic of Bosnia and Herzegovina expressly by use of that word. But in Paragraphs 51 and 52 of this second Order, the World Court did the next best thing:

The crime of "genocide" is a legal term of art that is based upon the existence of certain factual predicates as set forth in part by the General Assembly in Resolution 96(1) on "The Crime of Genocide." In Paragraphs 51 and 52 of this second Order the World Court found the existence of several facts necessary to constitute "The Crime of

Genocide" in accordance with the General Assembly's Resolution even though the Court was prevented at this stage of the proceedings from ruling that "genocide" itself had actually been committed by the rump Yugoslavia by using that precise word. In other words, as far as the World Court was concerned, Bosnia had already won this lawsuit on the merits and had only to continue through the merits stage of the proceedings in order to obtain a pre-ordained final Judgment on the merits in Bosnia's favor against the rump Yugoslavia for genocide.

In Paragraph 51 of the second Order the World Court expressly referred to the crime of genocide as something that "shocks the conscience of mankind, results in great losses to humanity...and is contrary to moral law and to the spirit and aims of the United Nations," quoting from the U.N. General Assembly Resolution 96(1) on "The Crime of Genocide." Then in Paragraph 52 the World Court does expressly make the finding of fact that "...great suffering and loss of life has been sustained by the population of Bosnia-Herzegovina." This language is stronger than "great losses to humanity" found in the General Assembly's Resolution on "The Crime of Genocide" that the Court had quoted in the immediately preceding paragraph. In other words, the World Court rendered a formal finding of fact that the predicate to the crime of genocide—"great losses to humanity"—had been exceeded by the "great suffering and loss of life" sustained by the Bosnian People.

Paragraph 52 then continued: "...great suffering and loss of life has been sustained by the population of Bosnia-Herzegovina in circumstances which shock the conscience of mankind..." Notice that the World Court used the precise language taken directly from the General Assembly's Resolution on "The Crime of Genocide" that the Court had quoted in Paragraph 51, and employed that language with respect to the Bosnian People. In other words, the World Court found the existence of a second factual predicate of the international crime of genocide by the rump Yugoslavia against the People and the Republic of Bosnia and Herzegovina: "...shock the conscience of mankind..."

Finally, Paragraph 52 concludes: "...great suffering and loss of life has been sustained by the population of Bosnia-Herzegovina in circumstances which shock the conscience of mankind and flagrantly conflict with moral law and the spirit and aims of the United Nations..." By comparison, the General Assembly's Resolution on "The Crime of Genocide" quoted in Paragraph 51 only requires acts of genocide to be "contrary to moral law and to the spirit and aims of the United Nations." Notice that the World Court found that the circumstances in Bosnia "flagrantly conflict with moral law," which language is much stronger than the General Assembly's "contrary to moral law." Certainly, the word "conflict" is stronger than "contrary" even without the modifying adverb "flagrantly," which was not even required by the General Assembly's Resolution on "The Crime of Genocide." In other words, the World Court had found that a third factual predicate necessary to establish the crime of genocide had been far exceeded with respect to the People and the Republic of Bosnia and Herzegovina.

The conclusion is ineluctable that in Paragraphs 51 and 52 of this second World Court Order of 13 September 1993 the World Court found that several factual predicates necessary to constitute the crime of genocide had been committed by the rump Yugoslavia and its surrogate Bosnian Serb armed forces against the People and the Republic of Bosnia and Herzegovina, and that the Serb atrocities against the Bosnian People had by far exceeded the threshold level for genocide set forth by the General Assembly in its Resolution 96(1) on "The Crime of Genocide." In other words, as far as the World Court was concerned, Bosnia had already won this lawsuit for genocide against the rump Yugoslavia. The conclusion is inevitable, therefore, that in the opinion of the World Court all that Bosnia must now do is to continue through the merits phase of the proceedings in order to obtain a pre-ordained Judgment on the merits that the rump Yugoslavia has indeed committed acts of genocide against the People and the Republic of Bosnia and Herzegovina, both directly and indirectly by means of its surrogate Bosnian Serb military, paramilitary, and irregular armed forces.

This second Order of 13 September 1993 was purposefully designed by the World Court to be even more of an outright pre-judgment on the merits of the issue of genocide in favor of Bosnia than was the first Order of 8 April 1993. In other words, the World Court was telling the entire world, and especially the member states of the Security Council, that the Court had essentially found that genocide was currently being inflicted by the rump Yugoslavia against the People and the Republic of Bosnia and Herzegovina, both directly and indirectly by means of its Bosnian Serb surrogates. Therefore, the World Court was deliberately saying in this Second Order that all 100+ states parties to the Genocide Convention as well as the member states of the Security Council, and especially its Permanent Members, had an absolute obligation to terminate this ongoing genocide by means of the immediate and effective implementation of its first Order of 8 April 1993.

Paragraph 53 of the 13 September 1993 World Court Order makes even more findings of fact that are conclusive on the infliction of genocide by the rump Yugoslavia and its Bosnian Serb surrogates against the People and the Republic of Bosnia and Herzegovina:

> 53. Whereas, since the Order of 8 April 1993 was made, the grave risk which the Court then apprehended of action being taken which may aggravate or extend the existing dispute over the prevention and punishment of the crime of genocide, or render it more difficult of solution, has been deepened by the persistence of conflicts on the territory of Bosnia-Herzegovina and the commission of heinous acts in the course of those conflicts;

The "grave risk" language quoted above was taken from Paragraph 45 of the 8 April 1993 Order, which was mentioned by the World Court in Paragraph 49 of the second Order of 13 September 1993 as follows: "49. Whereas in paragraph 45 of its Order of 8 April 1993 the Court concluded that there was a grave risk of acts of genocide being committed..." I have already pointed out why Paragraph 45 of the 8 April 1993 Order was tantamount to a pre-judgement on the merits of the case that the rump Yugoslavia had indeed inflicted genocide against the People and the Republic of Bosnia and Herzegovina, as conceded by the late Judge Tarassov in his Declaration of 8 April 1993.

By means of Paragraph 53 of the second Order, the World Court expressly stated that since 8 April 1993 this "grave risk" of "...the crime of genocide... has been deepened..." Once again the World Court was telling the entire world and especially the Permanent Members of the Security Council that the rump Yugoslavia was currently inflicting even worse genocide against the People and the Republic of Bosnia and Herzegovina than the Serbs had been doing as of 8 April 1993. Also, the World Court's reference to "heinous acts" only strengthened the conclusion that in the opinion of the Court the rump Yugoslavia was indeed committing even worse acts of genocide against the People and the Republic of Bosnia and Herzegovina. Finally, this Paragraph 53 also indicates that in the opinion of the World Court, the rump Yugoslavia had violated the provisional measure set forth in Paragraph 52B of its 8 April 1993 Order, inter alia.

Paragraph 55 of the 13 September 1993 World Court Order provides conclusive proof of the fact that the Owen-Stoltenberg Plan would have destroyed Bosnia's Statehood and robbed the Republic of Bosnia and Herzegovina of its Membership in the United Nations Organization:

> 55. Whereas the Security Council of the United Nations in resolution 859 (1993) of 24 August 1993 which, inter alia, affirmed the continuing membership of Bosnia-Herzegovina in the United Nations,...

At the very outset of the Owen-Stoltenberg negotiations in Geneva, on 29 July 1993 around 7:30 p.m. then Foreign Minister (later Prime Minister) Haris Silajdzic asked me to analyze the Owen-Stoltenberg Plan for President Izetbegovic. After working all night to prepare a formal Memorandum on the Plan for the President, and with a heavy heart, I informed Bosnia's Foreign Minister at breakfast around 8 a.m. Geneva time: "Briefly put, ...they will carve you up into three pieces, destroy your Statehood, and rob you of your U.N. Membership." At the end of our lengthy conversation, Foreign Minister Silajdzic instructed me: "You brief the press, I will tell the President!" Pursuant to his instructions, I immediately proceeded to explain to the world news media that the Owen-Stoltenberg Plan called for Bosnia to be carved up into three ethnically based mini-states, for Bosnia's Statehood to be destroyed, and for Bosnia to be robbed of its Membership in the United Nations Organization. I distributed my Memorandum dated 30 July 1993 to the world's news media in support of my conclusions.*

Several hours later, I received an urgent telephone call from Muhamed Sacirbey, Bosnia's Ambassador to the United Nations Headquarters in New York, asking me what he should do: "Convene an emergency meeting of the Security Council! Tell them they are stealing our U.N. Membership! Distribute my Memorandum! Try to stop it!" The net result of Ambassador Sacirbey's prodigious efforts in New York was Security Council Resolution 859 (1993) that guaranteed Bosnia's Membership in the United Nations despite the Machiavellian machinations of Owen and Stoltenberg in Geneva.

At the time everyone in Geneva knew full well that if Bosnia were to lose its U.N. Membership, then the Bosnian People would go the same way that the Jewish People did starting in 1939. Indeed, that was the entire purpose of the exercise in Geneva by Owen, Stoltenberg, and their lawyer Szasz: Implementing the "final solution" to the

---

*See Francis A. Boyle, *The Bosnian People Charge Genocide* 233-45 (1996).

inconvenient "problem" presented by the gallant resistance to genocide mounted by the People and the Republic of Bosnia and Herzegovina since March of 1992. But in the late summer of 1993 the Bosnians refused to go the same way the Jews did in 1939!

During the course of this second round of provisional measures proceedings before the World Court in July and August of 1993, I had requested the World Court to rule against the legality of the Owen-Stoltenberg carve-up of the Republic of Bosnia and Herzegovina on the grounds that this partition would subject 1.5 to 2 million more Bosnians to "ethnic cleansing," which I had already argued to the Court was a form of genocide. In response, the World Court did rule against the legality of the Owen-Stoltenberg Plan in Paragraph 42 of its Second Order by means of the following language:

> ...whereas, on the other hand, in so far as it is the Applicant's contention that such "partition and dismemberment," annexation or incorporation will result from genocide, the Court, in its Order of 8 April 1993 has already indicated that Yugoslavia should "take all measures within its power to prevent commission of the crime of genocide," whatever might be its consequences;...

In other words, by a vote of 13 to 2, the World Court effectively prohibited the Owen-Stoltenberg carve-up of Bosnia because it would result from acts of genocide, which were already prohibited by its 8 April 1993 Order. Nevertheless undeterred, thereafter Owen and Stoltenberg continued to plot their tripartite carve-up of Bosnia under the new rubric of the so-called "Contact Group Plan" with the full support of the United States, Britain, France, Russia, the United Nations, the European Union and its other member states.

In this second Order of 13 September 1993, the World Court then indicated that its first Order of 8 April 1993 was so sweepingly comprehensive that it did not need to be supplemented, but only "should be immediately and effectively implemented":

> 59. Whereas the present perilous situation demands, not an indication of provisional measures additional to those indicated by the Court's Order of 8 April 1993, set out in paragraph 37 above, but immediate and effective implementation of those measures;

Notice here the World Court's express finding of fact that the situation in the Republic of Bosnia and Herzegovina was "perilous." In other words, the rump Yugoslavia was currently perpetrating even worse acts of genocide against the People and the Republic of Bosnia and Herzegovina than the Serbs had been doing as of 8 April 1993. The very existence of the Republic of Bosnia and Herzegovina was in jeopardy.

Furthermore, it becomes crystal clear from reading through this second Order of 13 September 1993 that the World Court was indirectly criticizing the member states of the U.N. Security Council for having refused to fulfill their obligation "to prevent" the ongoing genocide in Bosnia. Pursuant to its own terms the World Court's first Order of 8 April 1993 was transmitted to the Security Council. The World Court noted in Paragraph 54 of the second Order of 13 September 1993 that the Security Council duly "took note of" its first Order in Resolution 819 (1993) of 16 April 1993. But the Serb acts of genocide against the Bosnians continued apace "...despite many resolutions of the Security Council of the United Nations..." to the great harm of the Bosnian People, as the World Court expressly found in Paragraph 52 of its second Order of 13 September 1993. In other words, in the opinion of the World Court, the Security Council had failed to adopt prompt and effective measures to terminate the ongoing genocide against the People and the Republic of Bosnia and Herzegovina, and especially despite its first Order of 8 April 1993.

In accordance with its own terms, this second World Court Order of 13 September 1993 was also transmitted to the U.N. Secretary General for transmission to the U.N. Security Council. It is obvious from reading through this second Order that the World Court was calling upon the member states of the U.N. Security Council to immediately and effectively implement its first Order of 8 April 1993 against the rump Yugoslavia in order to stop the ongoing genocide against the People and the Republic of Bosnia and Herzegovina. This the member states of the Security Council were required to do under the terms of both the Genocide Convention and the United Nations Charter. But despite this second, even stronger Order by the World Court on 13 September 1993, the Security Council and its Permanent Members refused to do anything to stop the Serb genocide and aggression against the People and the Republic of Bosnia and Herzegovina for the next two years until the Fall of 1995.

Article 31(3) of the Statute of the International Court of Justice provides: "If the Court includes upon the Bench no judge of the nationality of the parties, each of the parties may proceed to choose a judge as provided in paragraph 2 of this article." It was this author's decision to nominate Professor Elihu Lauterpacht of Cambridge University as Bosnia's Judge ad hoc in this case. Professor Lauterpacht is one of the leading Professors of Public International Law in the world today. He is also a man of great experience, integrity, and judgment. Finally, he is a distinguished member of the prominent Jewish community in Britain and thus, in my opinion, bore a special understanding for a race of people currently being victimized by genocide. Professor Lauterpacht had no prior connection with the Republic of Bosnia and Herzegovina.

By comparison, the Serb government nominated Milan Kréca to serve as their Judge ad hoc in this case. In accordance with his submitted resume, Mr. Kréca was a Serb lawyer who had worked for the Serb government. In other words, unlike Professor Lauterpacht, Mr. Kréca was not independent of the Serb government.

For this reason, at the time of Mr. Kréca's nomination by the Serb government to be their Judge ad hoc in this case, I repeatedly argued to the Deputy Registrar of the World Court that the President of the Court (then Judge Robert Jennings of Britain) should disqualify Mr. Kréca on the basis of his resume alone because he obviously was not independent of the Serb government. Eventually I was informed by the Deputy Registrar that the President of the World Court had taken the position that in the event I insisted upon my objection to Mr. Kréca's qualifications, there would have to be a formal hearing by the full Court on my objections and that this hearing would undoubtedly postpone the then scheduled World Court hearing on my Second Request for provisional measures of protection for Bosnia against the rump Yugoslavia that the Court had already ordered to take place on August 25 and 26, 1993.

Of course, under no circumstances could I risk jeopardizing that World Court hearing on my Second Request for provisional measures. It would be the only chance I had to stop the Owen-Stoltenberg carve-up of Bosnia into three pieces as well as to break the genocidal arms embargo against Bosnia. So I told the Deputy Registrar to inform the President of the Court that under these dire circumstances I had no choice but to accept Mr. Kréca as Serbia's Judge ad hoc, but that I protested his presence on the Court in the strongest terms possible.

It would serve no purpose here for me to analyze Judge ad hoc Lauterpacht's lengthy Separate Opinion attached to the World Court's Order of 13 September 1993. It speaks for itself, and--I might add--quite eloquently so. Nevertheless, within his erudite exposition,

I wish to draw to the reader's attention the critical passage found in Paragraph 102 of Judge ad hoc Lauterpacht's Separate Opinion:

> 102. Now, it is not to be contemplated that the Security Council would ever deliberately adopt a resolution clearly and deliberately flouting a rule of *jus cogens* or requiring a violation of human rights. But the possibility that a Security Council resolution might inadvertently or in an unforeseen manner lead to such a situation cannot be excluded. And that, it appears, is what has happened here. On this basis, the inability of Bosnia-Herzegovina sufficiently strongly to fight back against the Serbs and effectively to prevent the implementation of the Serbian policy of ethnic cleansing is at least in part directly attributable to the fact that Bosnia-Herzegovina's access to weapons and equipment has been severely limited by the embargo. Viewed in this light, the Security Council resolution can be seen as having in effect called on members of the United Nations, albeit unknowingly and assuredly unwillingly, to become in some degree supporters of the genocidal activity of the Serbs and in this manner and to that extent to act contrary to a rule of *jus cogens*.

In other words, Judge ad hoc Lauterpacht had pointed out for the entire world to see that the Security Council's arms embargo against the Republic of Bosnia and Herzegovina had aided and abetted genocide against the Bosnian People! Furthermore, Judge ad hoc Lauterpacht knew full well that his Separate Opinion would be transmitted with the Second Order of 13 September 1993 to the United Nations Security Council. Thus, Judge ad hoc Lauterpacht had purposefully and officially placed on notice the member states of the Security Council that their arms embargo against Bosnia was aiding and abetting genocide against the People and the Republic of Bosnia and Herzegovina.

During the early morning hours of 14 September 1993, the author rose to fly to Geneva for further consultations with President Izetbegovic, Vice President Ejup Ganic, and then Foreign Minister Silajdzic. It was my advice to all three that the next step for Bosnia and Herzegovina at the World Court would be to sue the United Kingdom for aiding and abetting genocide against the Bosnian People in order to break the genocidal Security Council arms embargo of Bosnia and to stop the genocidal carve-up of the Republic pursuant to the proposed so-called Contact Group Plan. This recommendation was taken under advisement.

Pursuant to the authorization of President Izetbegovic, on November 10, 1993 the author was instructed by Ambassador Sacirbey to institute legal proceedings against the United Kingdom for violating the Genocide Convention and the Racial Discrimination Convention in accordance with my previous recommendation. On 15 November 1993, Ambassador Sacirbey convened a press conference at U.N. Headquarters in New York in which he stated Bosnia's solemn intention to institute legal proceedings against the United Kingdom. Later that day, the author filed with the World Court a Communication that I had drafted, which was entitled *Statement of Intention by the Republic of Bosnia and Herzegovina to Institute Legal Proceedings Against the United Kingdom Before the International Court of Justice.* * Ambassador Sacirbey had also distributed this *Statement* at his press conference.

In this 15 November 1993 *Statement,* the Republic of Bosnia and Herzegovina formally stated its solemn intention to institute legal proceedings against the United Kingdom before the International Court of Justice for violating the terms of the 1948 Convention on the Prevention and Punishment of the Crime of Genocide; of the 1965 International Convention on the Elimination of All Forms of Racial Discrimination; and of the other sources of general international law set forth in Article 38 of the World Court's Statute. This 15 November 1993 *Statement* also indicated that the Republic of Bosnia and Herzegovina had issued instructions to the author to draft an Application and a Request for Provisional Measures of Protection against the United Kingdom, and to file these papers with the Court as soon as physically possible. Ambassador Sacirbey had this *Statement* circulated at United Nations Headquarters in New York as an official document of both the Security Council and the General Assembly.

On 30 November 1993, by telephone the author personally informed Ambassador Sacirbey in Geneva that these documents were ready to be filed with the World Court at any time. But by then it was too late. In immediate reaction to Ambassador Sacirbey's public *Statement* of Bosnia's intention to institute legal proceedings against the United Kingdom on 15 November 1993, a Spokesman for the British Foreign Office said that this announcement "would make it difficult to sustain

---

Francis A. Boyle, *The Bosnian People Charge Genocide* 365-67 (1996).

the morale and commitment of those [British troops and aid workers] in Bosnia in dangerous circumstances." This story continued: "Foreign Office sources said there were no plans to remove the Coldstream Guards, who have just begun a six-month deployment to Bosnia. But Whitehall would take account of whether the Bosnian threat of legal action was in fact taken to the International Court of Justice in The Hague."

In addition to the British government, several European states threatened the Republic of Bosnia and Herzegovina over the continuation of Bosnia's legal proceedings against the United Kingdom before the World Court in accordance with the 15 November 1993 *Statement*. The basic thrust of their collective threat was that all forms of international humanitarian relief supplies to the starving People of the Republic of Bosnia and Herzegovina would be cut-off if my Application and Request for Provisional Measures against the United Kingdom were to be actually filed with the World Court. For these reasons of severe duress and threats perpetrated by the United Kingdom, other European states, and David Owen, the Republic of Bosnia and Herzegovina was forced to withdraw from those proceedings against the United Kingdom by means of concluding with it a coerced "Joint Statement" of 20 December 1993.

Nevertheless, on the afternoon of Monday, 3 January 1994, the author called the Registrar of the International Court of Justice in order to make three basic Points to him for transmission to the Judges of the World Court:

1. The Bosnian decision to withdraw the lawsuit against the United Kingdom was made under duress, threats, and coercion perpetrated by the British government and the governments of several other European states upon the highest level officials of the Bosnian government in Geneva, London, and Sarajevo. Therefore the so-called agreement to withdraw the lawsuit against Britain was void *ab initio*. I reserved the right of the Republic of Bosnia and Herzegovina to denounce this agreement at any time and to institute legal proceedings against the United Kingdom in accordance with the *Statement* of 15 November 1993.

2. The British government demanded that the author be fired as the General Agent for the Republic of Bosnia and Herzegovina before the Court. The British government knew full well that the author was the one responsible for the Bosnian strategy at the World Court, and especially for the recommendation to sue Britain.

3.   Toward the end of my conversation with the Registrar on 3 January 1994, the author made an oral Request that the World Court indicate provisional measures, *proprio motu* in order to protect the People and the Republic of Bosnia and Herzegovina from extermination and annihilation by the rump Yugoslavia and the Republic of Croatia. I pointed out to the Registrar that this oral Request was in accordance with the terms of the written Request for provisional measures, *proprio motu* in advance that was already set forth in Bosnia's Second Request for Provisional Measures of 27 July 1993. The Registrar informed me that the Court was paying close attention to the situation in the Republic of Bosnia and Herzegovina.

Pursuant to Point 2, above, the author was relieved of his responsibilities as General Agent for the Republic of Bosnia and Herzegovina before the World Court on 12 January 1994.

On February 5, 1994, a mortar shell struck the marketplace in the center of Sarajevo, killing 69 people and wounding more than 200. The international outrage over this wanton atrocity inflicted upon innocent people by the Bosnian Serbs was so enormous that the Clinton administration was forced to seize the initiative for the so-called Bosnian peace negotiations from the United Nations and the European Union, and thus to take the matter directly into its own hands. The net result of this American effort was the Washington Agreements of March 1994.

The author analyzed the Washington Agreements in great detail in a *Memorandum of Law to the Parliament of the Republic of Bosnia and Herzegovina on the so-called Washington Agreements of 18 March 1994,* that I prepared and submitted to the Bosnian Parliament on March 24, 1994. This *Memorandum* is a public document that was considered by the Bosnian Parliament during the course of their deliberations over the Washington Agreements. It was originally published on the Bosnian Computer Newsgroup Bosnet (i.e., BIT.LISTSERV.BOSNET), and later elsewhere.

Instead of carving up Bosnia into three *de jure* independent states, the Washington Agreements prepared the way for carving up the Republic of Bosnia and Herzegovina into only two *de facto* independent states. One such *de facto* independent state—consisting of approximately 49 per cent of the Republic's territory—would be designated for the Bosnian Serbs, thus ratifying the results of their ethnic cleansing, genocide, mass rape, war crimes, and torture. The second such *de facto* independent state was actually created by the Washington Agreements and was called a "Federation" between the legitimate Bosnian government and the extreme nationalist Bosnian Croats working for separation at the behest of the ex-Communist apparatchik Croatian President Franjo Tudjman.

In theory, the so-called Federation was supposed to control 51 per cent of the territory of the Republic of Bosnia and Herzegovina. Nevertheless, it was clear from reading through the Washington Agreements that its American State Department drafters contemplated that ultimately this so-called Federation would be absorbed by the Republic of Croatia; and likewise, that the Bosnian Serb state would ultimately be absorbed by the Republic of Serbia. In other words, the Washington Agreements paved the way for the *de facto* partition of the Republic of Bosnia and Herzegovina between the Republic of Croatia and the Republic of Serbia. That had been the longstanding plan of Tudjman and Serb President Slobodan Milosevic to begin with, going all the way back to their secret agreement to partition Bosnia at Karadjordjevo in March of 1991.

The Washington Agreements of March 1994 became the basis for the drafting and the conclusion of the Dayton Agreement in December of 1995. Indeed, the Dayton Agreement can only be understood and interpreted by reference to the Washington Agreements. In other words, despite its public protestations to the contrary, throughout 1994 and 1995 the Clinton administration actively promoted and consistently pursued the *de facto* carve-up of a United Nations member state into two parts, and then Bosnia's *de facto* absorption by two other U.N. member states.

After imposing the Washington Agreements upon the Bosnian government, the Clinton administration then fruitlessly spent the next year and a half trying to convince Serbia and the Bosnian Serbs to go along with this *de facto* carve-up and absorption of 49 per cent of the Republic of Bosnia and Herzegovina. This would have required the Bosnian Serbs to voluntarily give up about 20 percent of the 70 percent of Bosnian territory that they had stolen and ethnically cleansed. That they proved unwilling to do until the use of military force against them by NATO in the Fall of 1995.

In the meantime, the siege and bombardment of Sarajevo and the other Bosnian cities persisted and the Bosnian Serbs continued to ethnically cleanse Bosnian towns of their Muslim and Croat citizens, with the active support and assistance of Serbia. The entire world watched and did nothing as the slaughter and carnage by the Bosnian Serb army continued relentlessly. This genocide culminated in the Serb massacres of thousands of Bosnian Muslims at the so-called U.N. "safe havens" of Zepa and Srebrenica during the Summer of 1995.

On September 8, 1995, the Clinton Administration imposed a so-called *Agreement on Basic Principles* upon the Bosnian government in Geneva as part of the run-up to Dayton. It was clear to the author that the Geneva Agreement constituted the next stage in the American plan to carve up the Republic of Bosnia and Herzegovina into two *de facto* independent states that had been initiated by the 1994 Washington Agreements. In order to warn the Bosnian Parliament of these machinations, I prepared a formal *Memorandum of Law to the Parliament of the Republic of Bosnia and Herzegovina Concerning the Agreement on Basic Principles in Geneva of September 8, 1995*, dated 11 September 1995. This *Memorandum* was submitted to the Bosnian Parliament and considered during the course of their deliberations. It was published on Bosnet on September 12, 1995.

At about the same time, it also appeared from published reports and from my own sources that the United States government was going to impose the partition of Sarajevo upon the Bosnian government as part of the so-called "final solution" for Bosnia. This is exactly what David Owen had planned to do in Geneva during the summer of 1993. In order to head off this partition plan, I prepared yet another *Memorandum of Law to the Parliament of the Republic of Bosnia and Herzegovina*, entitled *Saving Sarajevo*, dated September 13, 1995, and published on Bosnet, September 13, 1995. A Bosnian language translation of this *Memorandum* was published on Bosnet, September 24, 1995.

Briefly put, this *Memorandum* on Sarajevo resurrected the proposal that I had originally designed and drafted at the request of President Izetbegovic while serving as Bosnia's Lawyer at the Owen-Stoltenberg negotiations in Geneva during the summer of 1993: Turn Sarajevo into a Capital District like Washington, D.C., instead of partitioning the city. Although I was not at Dayton, as far as I can tell from the published sources, my proposal constituted the opening position for the disposition of Sarajevo that was presented by the Bosnian Government at the Dayton negotiations.

Fortunately, it proved unnecessary to implement my proposal at Dayton. For there the President of Serbia, Slobodan Milosevic, proved willing to concede a unified Sarajevo to the control of the so-called Federation on the grounds that President Izetbegovic "deserved it" for having courageously endured the three and a half year siege and bombardment of that capital city by Milosevic's surrogates. However, my proposal could still serve as a model for the organization of Sarajevo on a multi-ethnic basis as the capital of a reconstituted Republic of

Bosnia and Herzegovina at some point in the not-too-distant future.

On 26 September the Clinton administration imposed yet another "Agreement" upon the Bosnian government in New York in order to pave the way for the carve-up of the Republic in Dayton. Once again, in order to alert the Bosnian Parliament to these machinations, I drafted a *Memorandum of Law to the Parliament of the Republic of Bosnia and Herzegovina Concerning the New York Agreement of 26 September 1995*, dated September 28, 1995. This *Memorandum* was submitted to the Bosnian Parliament for their consideration and then published on Bosnet, September 29, 1995.

Next, His Excellency President Alija Izetbegovic asked me to analyze the first draft of the so-called Dayton Peace Agreement that was submitted to him by Richard Holbrooke. For obvious reasons, this *Memorandum of Law* is and shall remain private and confidential. However, several of my basic criticisms were incorporated into the final text of the Dayton Agreement. For example, it is a matter of public record that the first draft of the Holbrooke Plan would have constituted a *de jure* carve-up of the Republic of Bosnia and Herzegovina. That never happened!

After the public initialling of the Dayton Agreement, I was asked by then Bosnian Foreign Minister Muhamed Sacirbey as well as by the Parliament of the Republic of Bosnia and Herzegovina to produce an analysis of the Dayton Agreement for the purpose of their formulating a package of reservations, declarations and understandings (RDUs) to the Agreement. This was done by means of a formal *Memorandum of Law* by me that was submitted to the Parliament of the Republic of Bosnia and Herzegovina concerning the Dayton Agreement, dated November 30, 1995. This *Memorandum* is in the public domain and was published on Bosnet, December 1, 1995.

Pursuant to this self-styled Dayton Peace Agreement, on 14 December 1995 the Republic of Bosnia and Herzegovina was carved-up *de facto* in Paris by the United Nations, the European Union and its member states, the United States, Russia and the many other states in attendance, despite the United Nations Charter, the Nuremberg Principles, the Genocide Convention, the Four Geneva Conventions and their two Additional Protocols, the Racial Discrimination Convention, the Apartheid Convention, and the Universal Declaration of Human Rights, as well as two overwhelmingly favorable protective Orders issued by the International Court of Justice on behalf of Bosnia on 8 April 1993 and 13 September 1993. This second World Court Order effectively prohibited such a partition of Bosnia by the vote of 13 to 2. This U.N.-sanctioned execution of a U.N. member state violated every known principle of international law that had been formulated by the international community in the post World War II era.

Bosnia was sacrificed on the altar of Great Power politics to the Machiavellian god of expedience. In 1938 the Great Powers of Europe did the exact same thing to Czechoslovakia at Munich. The partition of that nation state did not bring peace to Europe then. Partition of the Republic of Bosnia and Herzegovina will not bring peace to Europe now.

On 11 July 1996—the first anniversary of the Srebrenica massacre of several thousand Bosnian Muslims by the Bosnian Serb army with the assistance of Serbia—the International Court of Justice issued a *Judgment* in which it overwhelmingly rejected all of the spurious jurisdictional and procedural objections made by the rump Yugoslavia against Bosnia's Application/complaint for genocide that the author had filed with the Court on 20 March 1993. The World Court had already rejected these same objections twice before in its Orders of 8 April 1993 and 13 September 1993. But under the Court's Rules of Procedure, the rump Yugoslavia was entitled to a separate hearing and decision on these preliminary issues alone. Nevertheless, despite the overwhelming merits of Bosnia's claims for genocide against the rump Yugoslavia, enormous pressure has been brought to bear upon the Bosnian government by the United States, the United Nations, the European Union and its member states, Carl Bildt, and Richard Holbrooke, *inter alia,* to drop this World Court lawsuit in order to placate Slobodan Milosevic. Why?

When I drafted all of the World Court papers for Bosnia and also when I orally argued the two sets of Provisional Measures before the Court in April and August of 1993, I was quite careful and diligent to file and plead as much material as I could that personally implicated Milosevic in ordering, supervising, approving and condoning genocide against both the People and the Republic of Bosnia and Herzegovina. I personally attacked and repeatedly accused him of primary responsibility for the genocide in Bosnia for the entire world to see and to hear. For this reason, it will prove to be impossible for the United States, the United Nations, and Europe to rehabilitate Milosevic once the World Court renders its final Judgment on the merits of the case in favor of Bosnia, which will inevitably occur unless prevented.

Bosnia has already won what is tantamount to two pre-judgments on the merits of the case in the World Court's Order of 8 April 1993 and the Court's Order of 13 September 1993, as conceded by the late Judge Tarassov in his Declaration attached to the first Order, and in his Dissenting Opinion attached to the second Order. In other words, under the leadership of Slobodan Milosevic, the rump Yugoslavia has indeed committed genocide against the People and the Republic of Bosnia and Herzegovina, both directly and indirectly by means of its surrogate army under the command of two individuals already indicted for international crimes in Bosnia: Radovan Karadzic and Ratko Mladic. Nevertheless, for almost four years the entire international community refused to discharge their solemn obligation under Article I of the Genocide Convention "to prevent" this ongoing genocide against the Bosnian People that was so blatantly taking place in the Republic of Bosnia and Herzegovina.

Hence, except for the Bosnians, everyone mentioned above wants this World Court lawsuit to disappear from the face of the earth. For they are all guilty of complicity in genocide. As this essay goes into print, it does not appear that Bosnia's lawsuit will survive much longer. If and when Bosnia is forced to drop its World Court lawsuit for genocide against the rump Yugoslavia, then the negation of the international legal order will be total and shameless. The so-called Western powers and the United Nations will have confirmed their complete moral bankruptcy and gross legal hypocrisy for the rest of the world to see everyday in the former Republic of Bosnia and Herzegovina.

But there is something that the People of Bosnia and Herzegovina can do about this situation: The Bosnian People must stand up as One and make it absolutely clear to the great powers of the world, and especially to the United States and to Europe, that under no circumstances will they withdraw their lawsuit against the rump Yugoslavia for genocide. This World Court lawsuit is the only justice that the Bosnian People will ever get from anyone in the entire world on this or any other issue!

If this lawsuit is withdrawn, then the rump Yugoslavia and its supporters around the world, together with the United States, the United Nations, the European Union and its member states, will be able to rewrite history by arguing that genocide never occurred against the People and the Republic of Bosnia and Herzegovina. All the great powers and these international institutions will then argue that the reason why Bosnia dropped its lawsuit for genocide against the rump Yugoslavia was because Bosnia was afraid of losing its World Court lawsuit. In this manner these great powers together with the United Nations and the European Union will be able to justify their refusal to prevent the ongoing genocide against the People and the Republic of Bosnia and Herzegovina for almost four years despite the obvious requirements of the 1948 Genocide Convention, the 1945 United

Nations Charter, and the two World Court Orders of 8 April 1993 and 13 September 1993.

As I have established in this paper, Bosnia has already won this World Court lawsuit. All that Bosnia must do now is to see this lawsuit through to its ultimate and successful conclusion. It is inevitable that the World Court will rule that the rump Yugoslavia and its surrogate Bosnian Serb armed forces have committed genocide against the People and the Republic of Bosnia and Herzegovina. At that time, the claims of the Bosnian People for genocide will be vindicated for the entire world to see and for all of history to know. After all that they have suffered, and endured, and accomplished, the Bosnian People owe it to themselves and to their children and to their children's children, as well as to all the other Peoples of the world and to their children and to their children's children, to prosecute this World Court lawsuit through to its successful conclusion.

MAY GOD ALWAYS BE WITH THE PEOPLE AND THE REPUBLIC OF BOSNIA AND HERZEGOVINA!